I EXISTED

I EXISTED

L.C. Markland

1603 Capitol Ave., Suite 310 Cheyenne, Wyoming USA 82001
1-888-980-6523 | admin@urlinkpublishing.com

URLink Print and Media is committed to excellence in the publishing industry.

Book design copyright © 2018 by URLink Print and Media. All rights reserved.

Published in the United States of America
ISBN 978-1-64367-040-9 (Paperback)
ISBN 978-1-64367-041-6 (Digital)

Drama
19.09.18

ACKNOWLEDGMENTS

As the old saying goes, "Behind every great man is a great woman." The same is true while composing a novel. "Behind every great author is a great friend." In the past four years, I have written ten novels. Through it all, my friends stepped in to read, proof, reread, and review my works. At times, they were bold and brash. They shared their perceptions and thoughts about my work. That was a difficult pill to swallow. Yet, in the end, they spared me from much heartache and embarrassment. Other times, they encouraged me to continue writing. They, like the author, wanted to know the ending.

These people deserve my utmost attention and respect. They are Shirley Rice Verhey (author of "Love Abounds More," and "If Pews Could Talk):" my wife, Judy Markland; friends Raymond Shook, Christine Payerle Hagenbaugh, Linda Smith, and Tesa Strausser (author of "Love Never Fails").

If there is any one person I thank, it is my mother. She is the driving force behind my writings. She passed away in 2003. She always wanted to write a novel, yet believed she lacked the education and experience to do so. As a child, she taught me the importance of literature. I owe much to her.

FOREWORD

Honestly, I do not know where to begin. There are many factors that prompted me to write "I Existed." The thought started when my first grandson was born. I have the privilege of caring for him on a regular basis. Holding him makes me realize the importance of life. It also reminds me of the sanctity of life. Each day, he brings and shows me new and simple things. His development outside the womb is nothing less than what occurs within the womb.

His birth, sparked on emotions I long forgotten, or I chose not to remember. Several years ago I became intimate with a young lady. Our paths crossed while in training. What started out as an innocent relationship became something much more. If truth be told, I was the aggressor. Prior to our chance encounter, I completed an operation that went terribly array. In the process of executing orders, several friends lost their lives. For whatever reason, I was spared.

Life, for me, meant absolutely nothing. I had no conscience. It was not until an old roommate contacted me when I learned of this young lady's fate. He informed me she ended her life along with her child's. Yes, she was carrying my child. I had no clue. Subsequently, my roommate questioned my character as a person, as a man, and as a leader.

In many ways, my friend was correct. Two lives were lost because of me. I tried to justify my actions but there was no excuse.

I deliberately misled a young woman: a young woman who cared. I was responsible for her demise as well as our child's.

While the birth of my grandson breathed new life in me, it does not negate the fact of who I was and what I did.

When I sat down to work on this work, I never realized the emotions fueled on by my research. On one hand, I came to appreciate the act of creation. I learned the dynamics of conception as well as a child's development within the womb. On the other hand, it drove the point home as to my personal culpability.

As such, I decided to tackle this issue on differing planes. "I Existed" is directed toward a teenage girl's response on learning she is with child. It moves toward other people's reactions. It looks deep into the heart of everyone involved. It is coupled and complicated by the laws governing and protecting the rights of some while ignoring the rights of others.

Hopefully, the novel entices the reader to rethink his or her position on life.

Personally, I was never a proponent of abortion. My stand has been, and always is, that all people have a choice. If they must choose, then they need to be responsible, accept the consequences and culpability for the decisions made.

Returning to my friend of long ago, had I known of her condition, I would have accepted full responsibility for the choices she and I made. Instead, she opted to terminate her life as well as our child. Never was I given the opportunity to prove myself. As the father, I was denied the right to raise my child. To this day, I must wonder what and how my life would have been different had I known the truth.

The birth of my grandson has definitively ignited my interests in this issue. Though most readers are left to conclude the conclusion of this work, I am sure my personal biases are brought to the forefront. But in the end, it is for the reader to decide.

CHAPTER ONE

This book is about Zachary Taylor and his life. Throughout the course of this work, you, the reader, will be introduced to certain aspects of Zachary Taylor's life. Many of the details described occur within his mother's womb, others are pertinent to the life God had intended for him.

Before I begin, please note Zachary Taylor was conceived out of wedlock. His mother, Carol, was nothing more than a senior in high school. Though she came from a lower-middle class family, she was extremely popular. Her athleticism, academics, coupled with her attractiveness, put her above the rest. She was hot! Yet, regardless of her popularity in school, she struggled with her personal identity. Her father was nothing more than a workaholic and alcoholic. If he was not serving his community as a second-rate citizen, then he was serving himself to a bottle of Canadian Club.

Her mother, Maria, on the other hand, was a woman of great faith. It was Maria's faith that kept her deadlocked in a dead-end marriage. Sure there were times she felt compelled to terminate the conjugal bonds that held her in bondage, but she feared excommunication from her church. Instead, Maria would always look for that silver lining in a thundercloud.

In her pursuit to keep the family glued together, everything seemed to unravel. Her husband's drinking intensified as well as his verbal assaults on Maria and Carol. Eventually, it was he who made the decision to vacate his responsibilities to the home. One day, he had enough. He had enough of working a job that led nowhere. He had enough of the demons that drained his will to fight. And he had enough of how drinking became his only resort. His only recourse was found in death. He came home from work, engulfed a fifth of whiskey, walked to his closet, pulled out his 38-special, went to the bathroom where he took aim and fired. Within a fraction of a second, he was finally at peace. His blood and brain matter splattered across the shower stall.

It was Carol who heard the shot and rushed to the scene. It was Carol who found her father's lifeless body. She tried to conceptualize and rationalize everything, but couldn't. All she could surmise was that she was to blame. Who could blame her?

For as long as she could remember, she was the source of her parent's problems. They were, of course, high-school lovers. As a result, they became emotionally, and then intimately involved. She was the product of a romance that happened so long ago. She was also the purpose her parents married. Had she not been conceived, things would have been different, or at least that is what she was told.

There in this still and sullen place, she sunk her back against the bathroom wall and sobbed. It was her fault. It was her untimely birth that ultimately led to her father's untimely death.

Maria found father and daughter in the bathroom. The former was dead. The latter wished she was never born. The guilt was too much for her to bear. Time and time again Carol heard her parents argue over their problems. Carol, by far, was the common denominator between them. Sure, Maria did all she could to comfort her daughter, but her words fell on deaf ears. Carol could not comprehend how both parents claimed to love her, yet hate one another because of her.

This is where Zachary's story begins. Unbelievably, it begins where another's life had ended.

CHAPTER TWO

The day of the funeral was wet and cold. The seasons were torn between summer and autumn. The air outside was heavy and moist. The sun tried to break through the overcast skies. Everything Carol experienced on that hallowed day represented every emotion she felt. Her heart was heavy. She was numb. Everything was nothing more than a blur. She remembered people talking, but she could not recall what they said. She wanted to be strong. She needed to be strong. Her mother looked to her for support. Her fellow students depended on her.

That night of all nights was the school's first dance. Carol was charged with orchestrating this event. Every detail was entrusted to her. Though school officials and students excused her from her responsibilities, Carol refused to accept their kindness. Besides, rumors ran rampant that she was "Queen." In all honesty, this annual dance would do her good. It would get her away from the home that created so much strife.

Besides, there was speculation that Frank, the high school quarterback, was to be crowned the "King." This and this alone gave Carol all the more reason to attend. For years, she and Frank were attracted to one another. They were, in heart and mind, secret lovers. Yet, the Continental Divide that spanned the gulf separated them.

Frank's family was from the upper echelon of society. His father was a reputable businessman and his mother was heavily involved in school politics. Unlike Carol's family, they were considered the elite. Never would they approve of Carol. In as far as they were concerned, she was nothing more than "trailer-park trash." If anyone should know, it was Frank's parents. They went to school with Carol's parents. They knew the tale of tales. Carol's father was an up and coming athlete while her mother was considered the catch of the century. She made heads turn. She made young men drool.

Their fate was determined by one decision. One fatal decision that changed the course of history for all involved. It was homecoming night. Maria stood before the student body as "Homecoming Queen." Carol's father, with the promise of an athletic scholarship from most colleges, was, you guessed it, the "Homecoming King." That evening, they failed. They gave in to their temptations, they had intercourse, and the rest was, as they say, history. Their lives were never the same.

Well, history has a way of repeating itself. No matter how hard one tries to rewrite the wrongs of yesteryear, those wrongs to tend bare their ugly face. It's human nature. What has mankind learned from the past? Nothing! Absolutely, nothing!

CHAPTER THREE

Despite that dark and dismal day, there was a silver lining. Ironically, it occurred during the hours of darkness. It all took place during the dance. Carol, as you guessed, was indeed voted queen, while Frank was named king. Together they stood hand in hand before the entire student body on stage. Once crowned, as is custom, they took to the floor.

Like a father holding his first-born child for the first time, Frank gingerly placed his hands on Carol's hips. In return, she draped her arms around his neck like a curtain on a rod. In sync, their bodies swayed to the music. The emotions they held in check for so long could no longer be sustained. She looked up into his eyes as he looked down into hers. They were spellbound. They were mesmerized. They were two magnets drawn to one another. There in the spotlight, with all to see, their lips met for the first time.

Whether it was the lights bouncing of the ball mounted above or the electrical charges within them, they did not know. What they shared was a power beyond description. By most accounts, it was the power of love.

Frank and Carol remained inseparable for the rest of that evening. Even when the lights finally dimmed and everyone was dismissed, they clung to one another. As a gentleman, he asked her to dinner followed by a romantic walk in a nearby park. Carol's initial response was to decline his offer. Her mother needed her. Not to mention, it was a scenario of yesteryear that that led to the tragic events.

Regardless of how hard she wanted to say "no," she couldn't. At that time and very moment, Frank held her heart in his palm. He knew it. What he didn't know was how history has a way of repeating itself.

He took Carol to one of the finest restaurants in town. There, they sat and talked. There they wined and dined. And it was there they finally and honestly opened their true feelings. It was a match made in heaven. So a person would think. But not all stories have a Cinderella ending. Yes, Frank found the crystal slipper, and yes, he drove the carriage. And of course, he found his Cinderella. After dinner, he escorted his damsel in distress to a local park.

With a full moon and the late summer air, their senses kicked into high gear. A gentle breeze gingerly swept over the treetops and across the pathways. The air kicked up the aroma of the season. Frank and Carol could smell the different fragrances the leaves had to offer.

Together they walked. They approached an opening. It was a field. At its end was a shelter. Nervously, he took her by the hand. He quietly guided her to the silhouette that lay hidden behind the moon's shadows. He paused. He used his free hand to point the various stars blanketing the night sky. He noted Orion's belt. He explained how the ancients were notorious for building great structures in line with the three stars. The pyramids of Egypt came to mind. He then directed Carol's eyes to Venus. He shared how it was the second planet from the sun. He went on to say how this particular planet was named after the Roman goddess of love and beauty. To add emphasis to its importance to the night sky, Frank went one step further. Outside of the moon, he explained, Venus was the second brightest object in the night sky.

Carol was impressed with his love for nature and astronomy. So much so, that she countered his romantic side by drawing his face ever so close to hers. Standing on her tip-toes, she raised her lips to his. He did not resist. He reciprocated. He swept her off her feet. He lifted and cradled her in his arms. He carried her across the field and laid her on a table beneath the shelter.

Nothing was said between the two. Nothing was asked. They let the stars guide their next move. There underneath the shelter and the stars, they let history repeat itself. They became vulnerable. They became intimate. They become one in more ways than one. Had they known what the stars dictated, things may have been different. But as fate always has its way, there were other bodies moving. Those bodies are not seen by the naked eye. They occur within the deepest parts of a person's soul. They travel silently until their alignment becomes clear. And so it was with Carol and Frank.

CHAPTER FOUR

It did not take long for gossip to run rampant through the high school. Some students reported seeing Carol and Frank in the local park. As a matter of record, they would swear under oath they witnessed the personal interaction between the two. While some found those rumors to be romantic, others found it repulsive. The lines were drawn between the two. Only time would bear the true fruits of what had taken place.

Sure, Carol and Frank did everything to thwart off any suspicions. Who could blame them? They were, of course, from the opposite side of the tracks. Frank knew the reality of his situation, and so to did Carol. They knew by societal standards they were not suitable. They also knew that while they attended the same school, the same popularity, and the same feelings toward one another, the odds were against them. Frank accepted an athletic scholarship to a Big Ten team. It seemed the course of his life was chartered. She, on the other hand, was still waiting to hear any news from any college.

These facts worked against them. Months passed since that night. Though Frank never forgot that one moment in time, it was nothing more than as a side step on his track in life. Sure, he respected Carol. If truth be told, he was in love with her. But his parents reminded him of the situation. She was born from a different breed. Life with her would be difficult and dangerous. Her father's death was a testimony to that fact.

Carol, on the other hand, had a different interpretation of events. She willingly gave of herself for the sake of love. Sure, some could argue that her actions stemmed from her father's death and they may even argue that she took advantage of Frank's status. The truth of the matter is that she truly loved Frank. The night that ball illuminated the dance floor and the stars electrified the evening sky exemplified her true feelings for him.

Her interpretation of that magical evening had far greater consequences. Yes, there was another life to be considered. You guessed it. She was with child. This is where Zachary's story began.

Month's had passed since that magical moment under the stars. Besides feeling loved in a way she never knew, Carol knew things would never be the same again. She was not sure what it was or how it would end. But this one thing she did know, life was created. For weeks she wandered the halls wondering what to do or say. While time had yet to prove her suspicions, she was confident. She was pregnant. She wanted to tell Frank, but then again, her father's death and the reason for his passing was still fresh.

Eventually, she had to face reality. It was four months since her last cycle. She went to a local pharmacy and purchased a pregnancy kit. The following morning, her suspicions were finally confirmed. She was not sure how to feel or what to feel.

On the one hand, she was with child. All the pain she suffered as a child from an unwanted pregnancy was erased. She knew this child would be different. Never would she permit her past to dictate the future. She would love this child. She would do everything to protect the child within her.

Yet, on the other hand, she feared the repercussions. What would her mother think? How would Frank's parents respond? More daunting was Frank's reaction. He, like her father, was on the fast track to success. Would he be willing to sacrifice his scholarship for his child? Would she forget how she offered herself to him? She was not sure which question hurt the worse. There was only one thing she did know. She would carry this child to term. And, if necessary, she would raise the life within her on her own.

She tried every possible trick in the book to hide the contents beneath her clothes. She wore loose clothes. Eventually, those tactics proved futile. The truth was beginning to take shape and form. The "baby bump," as it is called started to protrude. Everyone took notice, especially Maria. She was the first. Maternally, she had suspicions.

There were the hormonal changes Carol experienced shortly after the night beneath the stars. Carol did not quite seem herself. She was moody, nauseated, tired, and her appetite continued to increase. Those symptoms coupled with the pregnancy test Maria found in the bathroom's basket added up. The blood she found on the panties Carol wore to the dance made sense. It was the result of a first-time encounter rather than an early period.

Initially, Maria buried her instincts. She did not want to face the reality that Carol got trapped in the same cycle as she had. "Oh, how could she?" Maria thought. Carol knew better. She was, as a matter of fact, the recipient of an unwanted pregnancy.

With Carol's belly bumping out, Maria took action. She made an appointment for Carol to see a gynecologist. Maria ignored the obvious. Instead, she told Carol that it was routine for a young woman to periodically get examined. Carol had her apprehensions, but she was in no position to argue. She knew her mother knew.

Thankfully, the doctor was a female. She performed a routine examination. She was not sure if Carol wanted her mother present to hear the results. At first, Carol was reluctant but knew she could no longer hide the truth. It was, of course, revealing itself. She welcomed her mother's presence. She hoped her mother would be supportive. She prayed for her mother's approval. After all, they were grieving the loss of a loved one. Maybe, just maybe, Carol's pregnancy would work for good. It could fill the void and vacancy they shared.

She consented to her mother's presence. From that point on, the doctor went on to explain the stages of pregnancy, what to and what not to expect. Empathetically, she expressed the options available to her. Sympathetically, she encouraged her to carefully consider each choice and then make a decision.

CHAPTER FIVE

The ride home was torture for Carol. Maria failed to give Carol what she needed most. That is love, compassion, and some understanding. Instead, she received her mother's infamous silent treatment. When they finally pulled into the driveway, the ladies parted ways. Marie went to her room while Carol went to hers. Carol heard the door down the hall slam. She flung herself on her bed and sobbed. Her last recollection of that day came from her baby within. It kicked.

Her subconscious took her to that night when her child was conceived. She will never forget the passion she felt when Frank carried her across the dew filled field. From the time he gingerly placed her on the picnic table to the time he penetrated her inner-being, she was at peace. She surrendered her purity for the sake of love. She held onto that magical moment where life begins. The sensations followed by the emotions were ecstatic. Her imagination quickly shifted from her time with Frank to the lasting impressions he left behind.

She dreamt about the mysteries of conception. Whether it was her discussion with the doctor or her experience that evening in the park, she visualized the trajectory Frank's specimen traveled. As if narrated by a third-party person, the story went as such:

The last thing I remember was being ejected into a place unfamiliar. It was warm, wet, and dark. I fought for my very existence. I was not alone. In fact, there were thousands struggling to the same end. Many of them were either lost in the black abyss or trampled on by the others. Regardless, the majority of my comrades never made it to the desired goal. There was nothing I could to do to save them. It was a matter of survival. Everyone was in it for themselves. They, like me, were in the same predicament.

Drowned by the darkness, I swam. For some strange reason, I knew my purpose. I knew what had to be done. I understood what was at stake. Using nothing more than mere instinct to guide me and the strength I mustered, I fought my way through every obstacle. Sure, there were many times I believed my fate would be similar to the others, but I pushed on, pressed forward and persevered.

Having exhausted all my energies, I rammed into this soft cell of sorts. Though soft, it seemed almost impenetrable. I did everything to penetrate its outer core. I bobbed, I prodded, and I bored. After twenty-four hours of tedious labor, I finally broke through. What I experienced from the point on was nothing more than spectacular.

My entrance caused a causal chain of events. Electrical charges from every side and every angle sparked throughout this sphere. There were explosions of every kind. Things above me, below me, and around me started to split. I was pulled in every possible direction. So much so, that I was not only torn asunder but also became one with this phenomenon. "How could it be?" I thought. "How could I be equally divided, yet remain as a whole?" That was a question I was soon to learn but never experience.

CHAPTER SIX

Morning finally dawned. Carol desperately tried to wrap her mind around her dream. Was it a sign from God? If so, then what was God trying to tell her? She was not sure. Her maternal instincts kicked in. She beheld her belly and then with both hands held it. Again, she could feel the faint flutter of a kick. She smiled. "I will love you," she whispered. "I will protect you."

Her comments soon came under fire. The very moment Carol walked into the kitchen, Maria was quick to put Carol's words to the test. Maria's eyes pierced through Carol's. "So tell me you little tramp," she asked, "have you decided what to do?"

Carol did not hesitate to take aim and shoot back. "As a matter of fact," she confidently said. "I have. I will finish what I started."

Maria raised her eyebrows. Carol sensed her mother's discontent. It was confirmed by her next statement. "Is that so? And how in God's creation do you plan to do that?"

Hoping to gain some sympathy from her mother, Carol answered. "I don't know."

"Is that the best you can do?" Maria shot back. "You don't have a clue, do you?" Her eyes burned with anger. "Honestly, is that the best you can do?" She paused and then countered with, "You don't know!"

"What do you want me to do?" Carol shouted.

Maria fired another round. "I will tell you what I don't want." The pain of her past took control. "I don't want you to make the same mistake as I did."

"Is that how you see, Mom?" Carol cried. "I am nothing more than a mistake?"

"You know what I meant!" Maria shouted.

"I don't know anything anymore. Tell me, Mom, am I the reason dad decided to end his life?

"Oh, don't be such a drama queen! Your father loved you." Maria screamed. "He took his life because of me. I forced him into a position he could never win!" With those words, Maria held her head and slid her back against the wall.

Carol was somewhat beside herself. Somehow her mother diverted the attention away from Carol's condition to her own personal agony. "What are talking about? How did you force dad to do something?"

"You don't want to know! You don't need to know!" Still squatting, she turned her head toward her daughter and continued. "Remember young lady, I am your mother. I don't need to tell you anything."

"That is perfectly fine!" Carol strongly stated before she headed back to her room. "So who's being the drama queen now?"

In response, Maria sobbed uncontrollably. She saw the back of her daughter only to scream out, "What do you want from me?"

Carol's march came to an abrupt stop. She pivoted to face her now adversary. She pointed her finger at her foe. "I want you...no...I need you to be my mother instead of some self-serving bitch!" She did not give Maria the opportunity to a say a word. She continued the action she started seconds ago. She entered her room and slammed the door.

She tried to put the pieces together but couldn't. She did not know what was worse. Walking the school's hallways or spending time at home. Both situations presented their own challenges. All in all, there was no one she could turn to or trust. She thought about Frank. Clearly, he must know something. And how couldn't he? It's never every day a girl begins to show signs of maternity.

She reached for the phone. She started to dial his number when she remembered the football team was playing that day. They needed a win to advance to the state finals. Carol knew all eyes would be on Frank. He was, of course, the star quarterback heading to the Big Ten. She did not want to distract him from any future prospects.

Instead, she turned her attention to the internet. The doctor shared some interesting aspects of her pregnancy. She wanted to know more. She was amazed at what she discovered.

It was hard for her mind to grasp everything that had taken place in such a short time. She could not put her finger on it. But since that magical and mysterious moment, things were starting to take shape. Each day she discovered something new about her child.

Some weeks ago, his heartbeat started for the very first time. What an experience. From practically nowhere, it started to race. It has not stopped. She wondered what his fragile heart would experience. Would it melt at first-glance when he saw his mother? Would she protect him like her womb? Would she continue to care for his every need? She did not know. All she could do was hope.

WOW! She just thought of something. That something is called love. She was not sure exactly what that meant outside of the boundaries surrounding her, but it seemed so inherent to her. Her heart compelled her. She could only imagine her son falling in love and giving his heartbeat to another person.

Her mind traveled to a few months ago. Her recollection of her son's conception was too far, too wide, and too deep to describe. It was a night she would never forget. It was a night when she opened herself to the man she cherished and loved. Her son was conceived out of her love for his father.

Something told her his heart would be broken on more than one occasion. If she knew how it would break. The betrayal her child would endure was beyond belief. No one saw it coming.

For a moment or two, her heart stopped. She questioned Frank's feelings toward her. What if he did not share the same feelings for her as she did him? What if she was nothing more than another trophy for him to claim? The what if's were too much for her to bear.

To add to the weight already placed on her shoulders, her mother's words and warnings came to the forefront. "How did she force her father's hand?" She wondered. "Who did her father want to discard as a mistake: Maria or Carol? Was it the thought of her existence that led to his death?" Her joy quickly turned to despair. "What if she was the reason for her parent's unhappiness? What if she was nothing more than a mistake or a freak accident?"

Like shifting sand, her thoughts went from one extreme to the other. It was, however, something that needed to be discussed. Sure, Maria was her mother, but a crime had been committed. If Carol was to make a clear and concise decision, then she had to put her mother on trial. Carol would subpoena her to take the stand. There would be no judge or jury. There would only be Carol and her mother.

Carol strategized the appropriate time and place for this inquisition. At present, the feelings between mother and daughter were too raw to further investigate.

CHAPTER SEVEN

Carol refused to allow such thoughts to convolute her mind. She continued to read about her son's progress. His heartbeat was not the only thing that started to take shape. Something else happened. She noticed how other parts of his frame took root. Several holes were being planted. The first, she believed was his nose. You know, that part of the human body used freely to exchange air. It's what makes life possible. Oh, to think that someday he would be able to inhale the fragrances of the various seasons. It was beyond belief.

She recalled the many times she stood in the open air to breathe the different smells of spring or the freshly fallen leaves during an autumn day. How could she forget about the fresh air experienced during a cold winter's day? It was the kind of air that freezes the lungs. It rejuvenates the human spirit and renews the soul.

It was hard for her to conceptualize, but something told her that those smells would work in perfect harmony with her son's beating heart. They would excite his emotions all the while numb his very existence. They would generate feelings unlike any other. Carol smiled to think that someday her little boy would fall in love.

His mouth was also forming. It was the means by which he would verbally express his innermost thoughts. At first, it will form as an alarm system. It will notify his loved ones when he was in distress and in need of attention. More than likely, his siren would sound when he was hungry, tired, or when he needed to be changed.

It will be the portal that provides nutrients needed for him to live and grow. Initially, he would latch onto his mother's breast. It is she who would provide nourishment for the first few months of his life. His little mouth will cling to her. His very existence would rest on her breast.

Carol was excited to read how her child would break away from the comforts of her breasts and begin to eat solid foods. Eventually, he would learn how to form words and sentences. He would learn to communicate with those around him. It would be his mouth that would vocalize his thoughts, emotions, and feelings. He would interact with the world around him.

The same mouth used to utter the words "I love you mom," would also be used to declare his undying love for another. Someday, he will gingerly press his mouth against the person he loved. It is a concept far beyond Carol's comprehension. All she could do was reminisce about the first time her mouth touched Frank's. Though she never verbalized her feelings, she was confident he felt them. At that time, her mouth spilled out every emotion she ever experienced.

Sure, some could argue that it was her father's passing that made an indelible impression. Others may insist that it was nothing more than a teenage crush. Regardless of popular opinion, Carol knew the truth. That kiss, their kiss was born out of love: her love for him and Frank's love for her. The child she now carried exemplified their love.

The thought sent chills down her spine. She wondered if her unborn would ever share the same experience. She did not know. Would he be able to capture the true essence of what transpired? She did not know. All she knew was his future rested on her decision. Taking the quote from Shakespeare, she questioned his existence. To be or not to be was the question.

CHAPTER EIGHT

Carol stayed in her room for the rest of the day. Her mind drifted. She thought about her baby. Instinctively she knew she was carrying a boy. She knew his name would be Zachary Taylor. Considering all things, she believed that would an appropriate name. She thought about sharing the news with Frank and the lives were to embark on. She was certain he would not leave her to raise their child alone. In her mind, things were looking up.

She could not wait to see him on Monday. She would break the news then. Hopefully, his season as a premier high-school quarterback ended and they could now focus on their future. Maybe then, he would consider the possibility of owning up to what was his. He was, of course, the father.

Her meandering mind came to an abrupt halt. While Carol had made the decision to place Maria on the stand, it was Maria, of all people, who requested her daughter to sit in the hot seat.

"Carol," she said, "I need to speak with you."

Still fuming over the earlier confrontation, Carol was reluctant to see her mother let alone talk with her. "What is there to talk about?" she asked.

"There are some things I believe you need to know." Maria's demeanor had drastically changed. She went from being the "bitch" Carol claimed her to be to a mother who deeply cared. She sat at the dining table and waited. She heard the bedroom door slowly open and soon saw Carol standing near.

Maria patted the seat next to her. She invited Carol to come sit. Carol looked at her mother. She wanted to believe Maria cared. She needed for her to care. "What are you going to do?" she asked. "Are you going to bark at me some more?"

"No, I promise." Again Marie patted the seat next to her. "Please sit. Earlier you asked a question. I owe you an answer."

Carol proceeded with caution. She sat next to her mother. Maria reached out to take hold of her daughter's hand. She started to cry. She sobbed bitterly. She begged for her daughter's forgiveness. "I am sorry. I am so, so, sorry! Had I known, I would have done things differently."

Carol was dumbfounded. "Mom, what are you talking about? What would you have done differently?"

As a baby finds comfort in its mother's shoulder, Maria found comfort in her daughter's. Her tears flowed effortlessly. "This is not about me, this is about you," she said sobbing. "You must understand sweetheart, I was a teen too."

Carol's patience was running thin. "Mom, I don't understand. You are not making any sense."

"Oh, honey. I was the one who wanted to abort you." She paused to catch her breath. "Your father would have nothing of it. He promised to give up everything for me to keep you. I am the reason he took his life. You were right, I am a self-serving bitch."

"It took a moment for Carol to digest what her mother shared. "Mom," Carol shouted, "how could you?"

"Honey, it's not what you think. Times were different back then. An unwed mother was viewed as nothing more than trash. Your father did the noble thing. He spared my reputation all the while saving the life of our child."

"Mom," Carol pleaded. "Was I a mistake?"

"Absolutely not," Maria shared. "I loved you the very moment I held you in my arms. I am so thankful your father loved you so much that he gave up everything to ensure your safety." Maria had to stop. She released her hand from Carol's and held it against her mouth.

"Your father ended his life because of me, and not you. I don't want you to ever blame yourself for what we did."

For the first time, Carol saw another side of her mother. It was a side she longed for so long. Her mother did care. Her mother was compassionate. And her mother, above all things, was human. She hurt as much as her daughter. For the second time, Carol took on the role of a nurturer. This time she drew her mother's face to her shoulder and comforted her. "We will get through this Mom," she said. "We will get through this."

Carol spent the rest of the weekend rebuilding bridges with her mother. Finally, things started to make sense. The two talked for hours about everything and anything. Carol had a deeper appreciation for the sacrifices they made on her behalf. Though some questions were answered, there was one that hung in the balance. It haunted her. If she was the apple of her father's eye, as her mother claimed, then what prompted him to take his life? There were other options for him. What led him to such an extreme? Sadly, that answer would not be answered until some months later.

CHAPTER NINE

Monday could not come fast enough. Carol couldn't wait to tell Frank the good news. She imagined how he would receive her into his arms and how the school would revere her. She was, of course, carrying Frank's child. That alone should bump her among the school elite. This, to Carol, was a true fairytale of love and romance.

Unfortunately, not all fairytales have a happy ending. When she saw Frank standing at his locker with some friends, she rushed toward him. Her pregnancy was more noticeable this day than others. She decided not to disguise her baby bump. She was proud to be pregnant.

"Frank! she shouted, "Frank, we need to talk." Everything from that point appeared to go in slow motion. Students parted the hallway as she ran with her belly in hand. Some pointed at her and others laughed at the sight. It was not every day that a pregnant girl ran through the school.

The moment Frank turned to face her she knew their conversation would not end well. It was written on his face. He was reeling from Saturday's loss. He was responsible. He threw four interceptions and now his scholarship to the Big Ten was in jeopardy.

He took one look at her "baby bump," and ended the discussion before it started. "No! No! No!" He blurted out. "Don't you even dare tell me it's mine, not now or ever!" Silence took over the student body. The finger pointing and laughter stopped. Everyone placed their hands over their mouths. Like Carol, they were in shock.

Carol cried out, "But I thought you…"

Frank prevented her from spitting out another word. Her voice was drowned by his and so too were her dreams. "You thought wrong! You are nothing more than a two-bit tramp. Do yourself a favor and get an abortion!" He turned, slammed his locker, smacked a nearby friend on the arm and said, "Let's get out of here."

Carol fell to the floor. She, like the child within her, curled into a ball. She bawled. Some friends came to her aid. They did their best to comfort and console her but to no avail. One of Carol's friends, Lucy, looked in the direction Frank headed and shouted, "You are an asshole!"

A counselor approached the scene of the wreck. It took him a moment to access the damage that now lay on the floor. "Okay, everyone, give Carol some air. I need you to go to your respective classes."

Lucy again spoke out for her friend. "Let me guess, you want Carol to go to? Are you as dumb as you look! Can't you see she is hurting?"

"That's enough," the counselor said. "You already have earned one detention. Would you like another?"

"A detention," Lucy argued, "for what?"

"If I am not mistaking, you did call me an 'asshole' a few moments ago."

"You are dumber than you look," Lucy said.

"That's two detentions, would you like a third?"

"No! I don't even want one," Lucy barked. "I didn't call you an asshole, I was calling Frank one."

The counselor chuckled. "You may have a point about my appearance then." Looking at Lucy, he went on to add, "You need to now go to your class. I will take Carol to the office."

"She didn't do anything."

"I know that. I will get her settled down and send her home for the day. Does that answer further concerns you may have?"

Lucy thought for a moment. "I guess not…well, I do have one. Must I serve three detentions?"

"I will make a deal with you," he said. "If you quietly return to the classroom, I will give you a pass on the three. Don't thank me now, just go." Lucy did as instructed. She left Carol in the counselor's care.

The counselor helped Carol to her feet and walked her to the school office. He noticed her bump. His heart melted as she sobbed her way down the hall. She was numb. She was dumbfounded. A day that held so much promise quickly ended in so much pain.

The counselor was well aware of her father's death. He knew she needed a father figure. He shielded Carol from those in the office. She suffered enough embarrassment for the day. He asked one the secretaries to write a permission slip for Carol to return home.

He took Carol into his office, closed the door, and suggested she take a seat. In a very calm voice, he asked, "When is your baby due?"

Drying the tears from her eyes, Carol answered his question. "He is due in June."

The counselor was surprised. "Oh, you already know the baby's sex?"

With a faint smile, Carol said, "It has not been confirmed yet. You know, it's a mother's intuition."

"It sounds like you are going to be a great mother. Do you have a name for him?"

Her eyes beamed with joy. "Zachary Taylor."

"I like that name. Zachary Taylor." The counselor paused for a moment. "May I ask who the father is?"

The beams that once illuminated her eyes disappeared. She shook her head in disgust. "Frank! I cannot believe he reacted the way he did. I thought he loved me."

"What did he do?"

Carol stared at her counselor. "What does it look like?" She thought about Lucy's description. "Maybe he is as dumb as he looks."

"My apologies," he said, "that was the wrong choice of words." He stopped and laughed out loud. He openly expressed what Carol thought. "I guess Lucy was correct. I may be dumber than I look." With that statement, this counselor started to build a bridge. "What did he say to you this morning?"

The floodgates opened again. Carol burst into tears. To even think about what that asshole said hurt.

"Take your time. You don't have to tell me if you don't want to."

She held out one hand as if to ask for permission to clear her thoughts. She used the other to cover her face. "No," she whispered, "I will tell you." After a few moments, she opened up. "He did not even give me a chance to say anything. He looked at my stomach. He accused me of being a tramp in front of everyone. And then he told me to get an abortion."

"Now I understand what prompted Lucy to call him an asshole. Have you decided on what to do?"

"Are you suggesting I abort my baby?"

"Absolutely not," the counselor said. "I was thinking more along the lines of finishing school, the means to raise this child, Zachary Taylor, and whatever future plans you have."

"No," Carol said tearfully. "I was waiting to tell Frank first. Apparently, he does not share the same feelings as I."

"I am not defending Frank, by any means. I will say, it must have been a shocker for him. And with so much riding on his shoulders for an athletic scholarship, he probably felt blindsided. If you want, I will talk with him."

"Yes, I would appreciate it."

"It's no problem. I will also talk with the other students regarding this morning. The last thing you need is to have more stress placed on your shoulders. We want Zachary Taylor to be a healthy baby. I am sending you home for the remainder of the day. Get some rest and try to relax. Everything will work out."

"Thank you," Carol said and then added. "Can I talk with you from time to time? I know I will need someone in the months to come."

The counselor assured her that his door was always open to her.

Before she walked out, her smile returned along with her eyes beaming. She respectfully looked at her counselor only to assure him that he was not as dumb as he looked.

CHAPTER TEN

Carol walked home. She tried to forget about what happened. She wanted to focus primarily on her baby. It was a beautiful day. In the late autumn sky, the sun made its presence known. It illuminated everything around her. The leaves whistled in the gentle breeze and showcased their colors as the rays of the sun pierced through every leaf. All was calm and quiet. That is until she started up her driveway.

Maria was getting into her car. It was her first day back to work since her husband's death. Like her daughter, her mind was preoccupied. In fact, she was nervous to return. She knew everyone in the office would treat her as if she had an infectious disease. She was scared. To complicate matters, her daughter was pregnant. She remembered what it was like to be a pregnant teenager. She also knew her husband ended his life because of a decision they both made in high school.

She was shocked to see Carol advancing. "What are doing home?" she asked.

"It's nothing Mom. I really don't wish to discuss it." Carol pleaded.

"He ditched you, didn't he?" she shouted out loud.

"Please, Mom; I don't want to talk about it." Carol tried to make her way to the house when Maria figuratively stabbed her in the back. "I told you what you should do! I will make an appointment as soon as I get to the office."

The hormonal imbalance in Carol showed. So did the events at school. Carol turned to face her mother. "You can be such a BITCH! Is it any wonder dad decided to take his life?"

The sun that once illuminated the sky now lay hidden behind the clouds. Things got dark. The wind picked up and Maria went sailing toward her daughter. Toe to toe mother and daughter stood. Maria pointed her index finger in Carol's face. "Don't you ever talk to me like that? Do you understand me? What in the hell did you think was going to happen? You and your boyfriend would run off and live the happily ever after. You are kidding yourself. He will drop you in a heartbeat. Something tells me he has already. ABORT this child before it gets out of hand!"

"Go to hell Mom," Carol cried out in anguish. "I'm keeping my baby."

Maria raised her hand to slap her daughter. She stopped when Carol screamed, "Now you are going to slap me? That's great Mom! What are you going to do next: cut my baby from my womb?"

The hand lowered. Maria knew she crossed the line of the great divide. "I need to go to work. Do whatever you want. I don't care anymore."

Carol had to have the last word. "That's right Mom. Turn your back and walk away. That is something you are good at." She slowly opened the door to the house. It was empty. Everything seemed so dark. Ever since her father's death, things would never be the same. She walked slowly and silently. She did not want to wake up any lingering spirits. She entered her bedroom. She removed her shoes and lay in bed.

She stared at the ceiling. She started to rub the life that lived within her. Her thoughts started to drift. She wondered if her "Little Zach" could talk what would he say. Somewhere and somehow she was in a trance. She envisioned herself inside her womb. She was next to her son. He spoke to her.

"*Mommy,*" he said. "*Things in here are rapidly progressing. Just this morning I noticed limbs starting to protrude from my outer core. Once fully developed, they will serve as my arms and legs. They will work together in perfect harmony. They will be my agents for progress.*

They will give me the mobility to move fast and forward. They will catapult me to explore new adventures. They will give me the freedom and flexibility to live life."

"At the end of each extremity are paddle-like shapes. I suspect they will ultimately become my hands and feet. Excitement fills me to know how they will be instrumental in directing my paths. My hands will be vital in so many ways. With them, I can hold onto those things most dear to me, such as your embrace, the bottle that feeds me, the ball I will someday throw, and possibly the person I am to claim as my own. My feet will give me the ability to stand firm, to walk and run forward, to jump ahead, and to back off and away."

"Outside of the externals, there are the internal aspects of my growth. My brain continues to develop. In fact, both hemispheres of my brain are taking shape. My liver, pancreas, and kidneys are developing. Everyday Mommy, I experience something new about myself. Please let me live the life I was meant to live. Mommy, I exist."

Carol reached out to take hold of her baby. Her trance was abruptly broken by someone banging on the front door. "Who could that be?" she thought. She left her place of refuge. She opened the door and found Lucy standing there.

"What are you doing here?" she asked. "Shouldn't you be in school?"

"You would think, but I received a three-day suspension," Lucy said. "I am in so much trouble when I get home."

"Tell me what happened?"

"Well, I got in a fight during lunch," Lucy countered.

"Who did you get in a fight with?" Carol's curiosity got the best of her.

"I will give you one guess. Who do you think?" Lucy proudly said.

It took Carol a moment or two to figure out who Lucy's sparring partner was. "No!" she shouted. "Tell me you did not!"

"Your damn right I did. That asshole was talking smack about you to his friends. I told him to either shut his mouth or I would shut it for him."

"And then what happened?"

Lucy smirked. "Well, he stood up and told me to take my seat with the rest of the tramps in the cafeteria. I'm sorry but no man will ever talk to me or about my friends in that fashion. I punched him in the mouth. He didn't know what hit him."

"And..?" Carol wanted to hear more.

There was a long sigh. "That was a far as it went. Thankfully, our counselor friend, you remember, the one who is dumber than he looks, pulled me away before things really got ugly."

Carol laughed out loud! "I wish I could have been there to see his face," she paused. "Hey," she went on to explain, "something miraculous happened to me. I saw my baby He spoke to me too!"

"I know you did, silly. You had an ultrasound, didn't you?" Lucy looked puzzled.

"Yeah, I did," Carol shared. She could sense that this was not the time or place to give details about her vision. "Anyway, I have decided to keep him," she said with much enthusiasm.

Lucy was glad to hear about her decision. Carol needed something concrete in her life. After all, she endured the pain of her father's passing; she could use some good news. "That's great. I am so happy for you. Do you think I can stay over awhile before I go home?"

"That is not a problem."

There both girls stood supporting the other.

CHAPTER ELEVEN

Carol woke up the following morning. She was excited. She made the decision to walk that road even if it meant she walked it alone. The disappointment from the previous day was behind her. She recalled her encounter with "Little Zach," as she called him.

She was ill prepared for what awaited her. This day, like the day before, was about to spiral out of control. In the end, Carol would find herself walking the road alone. Her decision would be put to the test. She entered the school where her counselor greeted her. She hoped his presence was a good thing. She was sadly mistaken. "Carol," he said apologetically, "I need you in my office."

"Did I do anything wrong?" She was confused. She wondered what would prompt an office visit.

"No, you did not do anything wrong," the counselor said assuredly. His words did not agree with his body. His face was tight. He was tense. And he started to sweat with each passing step. "I want to forewarn you, though: other people are waiting for us."

"Who is there?"

The counselor refused to answer her question. He was not fond of what was to transpire and how it was to transpire. "You will know soon enough," he mumbled under his breath.

With Carol in tow, the two entered his office. He closed the door. Sitting around a table were Frank's parents, her mother, and

Frank. Carol stopped dead in her tracks. She looked at the people in the room. It was evident she was caught off-guard. She trembled in fear. "Must I really be here?"

"I am afraid so," the counselor said. "It seems that every one present has a vested interest in you, Frank, and the baby."

"No, no they don't," Carol cried out. "They want me to dispose of him as if he never existed. Well, he does exist, and I am going to keep him." Carol darted for the door. Her counselor stopped her. He stood between Carol and the outside world. She tried to push him aside. He was not budging. He restrained her from making any advancement. With tears in her eyes, she looked into his. "I thought you wanted to help me! You lied! You are no different than the rest of them!"

She tried to make another advance to freedom, but to no avail. The counselor held her tightly. "I can't let you leave," he said apologetically. "I am bound by law to do what is in the best interest of my students."

Carol's attitude shifted. She went from being a pregnant adolescent to a professional attorney. "That's fine," she snouted. She turned to her jury of peers and went on. "I am glad you mentioned the law. By law, I am an adult. I have every right to make my own decisions. I have decided to keep my baby. There is nothing you can do to legally stop me."

Maria pulled away from the table. She stood up to give her rebuttal. "You are correct. The law says that it is your choice. You can decide to do whatever you want with your child." She refrained from completing her thought. She walked toward her daughter with open arms. She then calmly continued. "The law also says I am your mother. As your mother, you are my responsibility. I love you, Carol. I want what's best for my little girl. Honey, this isn't it!"

Maria's gesture of reckoning wrecked. Carol refused to accept her mother's comfort. She slapped her mother's hands and ordered her mother to get away from her. She shouted, "Whose side are you on?"

"I am on your side. That's why we are here. There are some things you need to know." She addressed the counselor. "If you don't mind, we need your office. I believe we can take it from here. Thank you."

The counselor stepped out. Frank stood from his seat and faced Carol. For a young man who had his fair share of hits, this was, by far, the hardest. His tears melted her heart. "I apologize for yesterday. I was wrong for what I said. I should have manned up to what we had and have."

Carol started to speak, but as the day before Frank stopped her. "Look," he said, "before you say anything please hear what our parents have to say. God forgive our parents for what they caused. I am so, so sorry for what I have done."

Carol was stupefied. "What are you talking about?"

It was Kelly, Frank's mother who took the floor. She drew a deep breath and wiped her tears. "Carol," she said sobbing. "I know you are angry with your mother, so please listen to me. There is the reason why we are so adamant about your pregnancy. Though we have kept our distance from you and your family, it had nothing to with status." Kelly could not contain her emotions.

She, like Maria, walked toward Carol with her arms open. Unlike Maria, she was received with extended arms. "We owe it to you and Frank. You need to know the truth." She buried her head in Carol's shoulders and sobbed uncontrollably. "I ask you and Frank to forgive us for what we did and how you must now suffer for the decisions we made."

"What are you talking about? Forgive you for what?" Carol tearfully pled.

She looked Carol directly into her eyes. Though she felt shame, she found strength. For once, she was going to tell the truth. It was the truth that would set so many free: so many except Carol. She cleared her throat. "You and Frank share the same father. You are brother and sister."

"Is this a sick joke?" Carol blurted out. In hurt and haste, she pushed Kelly away. "Get the fuck away from me. I don't believe you! You will do anything for me to abort my child!"

Maria intervened. "Carol! That's enough. Don't you dare use that language!"

"Mom, are you serious? Is my language the only thing you are worried about or is it that I got pregnant because I fucked her son?

Tell me Mom, which is it? Am I an embarrassment to you?" Carol felt alone. She felt abandoned. She felt betrayed. She tried to escape, but there was nowhere to turn.

Suddenly, the door opened. It was the counselor. He heard the commotion and believed it was his time to intervene. Besides, he was never in favor of this meeting in the first place. Politely and calmly he asked everyone to take a seat, take a breath, and to relax. There were issues he needed to discuss with all parties.

CHAPTER TWELVE

The counselor took his seat behind the desk. He waited for the air to clear. Once he believed everyone had some time to gather themselves, he spoke. "We have a problem," he said. "As a counselor, I am responsible for the student body. Since yesterday, they have seen an altercation in the hallway, followed by an assault in the cafeteria. I hoped this morning's meeting would quiet the storm. At present, that does not seem possible. Therefore I have no choice but to remove Carol from participating in school activities."

There was silence. He first wanted to see and then waited to hear from those at the table. It was Carol who first spoke first. It was one thing to be shamed before her peers, but to be suspended from them was a different matter. Though there was sympathy, there was by no means any empathy. "Why must I be the one to suffer?" she yelled while holding her abdomen. "What did I do to deserve this?"

She raised her one hand and pointed her finger at Frank. Her eyes burned with anger. "What price does he have to pay? Why does he get off so easy?" No one could argue with her. She was right. She was not the only person who saw the injustice in the decision.

Maria popped from her chair. "You have to be shitting me!" she declared. "Carol is not the only person involved in this affair. Dammit! She did not get pregnant on her own. What plans do you have for the father?"

Kelly then jumped into the debate. "You leave Frank out of this. He has a future don't you know? Besides, if your daughter would not have followed in her mother's footsteps, we would not be here, now would we?"

"You have room to talk, now don't you bitch? I was carrying Carol before you enticed her FATHER! You are more to blame for this than anybody."

"How dumb can you be?" Maria argued. Tempers were beginning to flare. Sadly, no one bothered to intervene. Whether they were mesmerized by what would be said next, or they were just being men, no one knew. "He loved me more than he ever loved you. We would be together today had it not been for you!"

Carol couldn't believe what she was hearing. She was confused enough. Her confusion was compounded by the mother's dialogue. "Mom, what are you two talking about?" Looking at Frank's mother and then Maria, Carol finally understood. Both women were in love with the same man. "You two weren't joking! How could you?" she screamed. "You mean I gave myself to my brother. Now I am with his child."

Maria was oblivious to the reason for this meeting. Her mind traveled back in time. From all appearances, she resembled a teenage girl. "Carol," she shouted. "This has nothing to do with you. It has everything to do with me and that bitch standing there! You think I didn't know about your affair? Common, do I look that stupid? To bang my husband in our bed! You could have at least had your fling at some cheap hotel!"

Kelly could not believe what transpired. In defense of Carol, she shot back. "Maria! Did you hear what you said in front of your daughter? This has nothing to do with us. It's about the welfare of your daughter and my son!"

Maria remained transfixed between the two states of consciousness. "Like hell it does! You are the reason for all of this. My husband killed himself because of you! You couldn't let good enough be alone! Oh no, you had to be the whore everyone claimed you to be. I will never forgive or forget what you did to me."

"And you," Maria fixated her eyes on Frank's father. "If you would have been half the man you say are, you would have put an end to it!"

Carol flung her arms in the air. She could not tolerate any more crap from either woman. She turned to her counselor. She begged, "Please, please say I can leave now. I won't return to school if you wish. I promise."

The counselor sat still. He did not know what to say, but he knew what to do. He nodded. He conceded to Carol's request. She did not have to ask twice. The moment his head took its first bob, she headed for the door. Again, silence filled the room. Maria followed her daughter to the door. She deliberately walked by her adversary. She paused and leaned over. "This is far from being over bitch," she whispered in her ear. With that, she exited.

CHAPTER THIRTEEN

Maria stormed out of the school. She got in her car. Instead of looking for her daughter, she drove home. Her emotions personified the weather outside. She was cold, and the winds that blew were ruthless and relentless. She entered her house to get ready for work. She looked in the mirror. The reflection staring back at her was ragged. She reached for her brush and murmured to herself. "I can't believe her. She is such a bitch!" She paused for a second. One would assume she reconsidered her daughter's affairs. That was not the case. She remained focused on her anger. She thought, "How in the hell does anyone expect me to go to work looking like this?"

Finally, she shared her true feelings. Even she was tormented by what flowed from her lips. "I knew I should have aborted her when I had the chance." The wind blew the front door open. The air whistled through the house bringing her back to reality. Loneliness was now the image glaring at her. She cupped her hands over mouth. It dawned on her the true extent of her anger. "Carol! Where's Carol?"

She went to close the door, only to find Frank standing on the threshold. Quietly she asked, "What do you want young man?" She saw the concern on Frank's face.

"I want to know how Carol's doing. Is she home?"

Maria started to cry. "I don't know. What business is it of yours? Don't you think you have done enough damage?"

Frank stood firm. He refused to vacate the premises until he knew Carol's condition. "Is she home?" he demanded.

"I told you, I don't know. But if you must insist," she snidely said, "I will go check."

"I would appreciate it. Thank you."

Maria went to Carol's room. It had not changed since earlier that morning. Carol's absence was the only difference. She returned to Frank. "I am sorry, but Carol is not home. Do you know where she might be?"

"I have my suspicions. With all due respect and your permission, of course, can I be the one who gets her?" Maria overlooked and underestimated Frank's character and his charm. His eyes were the portal to his soul.

Her demeanor changed. She became more subtle. Softly she answered. "Yes, you may. When you find her, please bring her home."

He politely affirmed and acknowledged her wish, "Yes ma'am, I will."

"Thank you," she said. She then closed the door before her and went to the bedroom behind her. Her emotions finally caught up with her. Her only recourse was to pray. She removed the cross from the wall it hung. She clung to it and fell to her knees. She first looked to the heavens and then bowed her head. With a heavy heart, she sought repentance.

CHAPTER FOURTEEN

Frank drove directly to the place where it all started. It was the park. It was the place where life was conceived. He walked the same trail he and Carol did on that special night. He came to the field's opening. He looked to the shelter. He saw a person sitting on a picnic table. It was the picnic table. It was Carol. Her back was facing Frank. Slowly he walked across the open plains. The wind had somewhat died down and the sun tried to find cause to break through the clouds.

She did not know of Frank's presence. She believed she was alone. Frank was not exactly sure how to tackle this situation, so to speak. He noticed Carol holding onto what appeared to be a picture of sorts. Gently, he sat next to her. She was startled when he softly asked what she was holding.

"It's the ultrasound of our child," she said.

"May I see it?" he asked. He stared at it for some time before saying anything else. It was difficult to make out. He tried to break the tension with humor. "Well, I guess there is no denying it, the baby looks like me."

His tactic worked. Carol chuckled. "Lucy was right, you know. You are an asshole."

Frank laughed. "Yes, I have been told that a time or two. By the way, your friend has a pretty good punch. Don't worry; I deserved everything she handed me." While the picture was nothing more than a blur, there was one aspect that caught his attention. It stood out from among the rest. He pointed to it. "Could you tell me what this is?"

Carol looked over. She smiled. "It's our child's heart."

Bewildered Frank was. "Is it beating?"

"Yes, yes it is beating. It beats 150 times per minute. He's alive. He exists!"

Speaking of heartbeats, Frank's heart started to race. More importantly, his heart started to change. He began to feel what Carol felt. "WOW! That's incredible." He stopped his train of thought. A lightning bolt struck his innermost being. "You are having a boy." The mere thought of having a son resonated well with him. "Are you sure?"

Carol gazed into his eyes. They were the same eyes as the night when they consummated their love. They were deep and they were as blue as the sea. They sparkled with life and love. "Yes, I am very sure."

"Do you have a name for him?"

"His name is Zachary Taylor."

Frank ran his finger over the image. "Zachary Taylor, I like it."

"I am glad you approve. I am keeping him." Carol confidently shared.

"I believe you made that clear this morning. Speaking of this morning, wasn't that crazy? I guess buried secrets will eventually be unearthed." Frank could sense the effects that meeting had on Carol. "It went far beyond crazy, don't you think? It did explain some things, I guess."

Carol snatched the ultrasound from Frank's hand. She bowed her head. "I suppose. Regardless, I am still keeping him."

"I know," he said. He put one arm around her shoulder and used the other to direct her face to his. "I love you, Carol. I always have. It doesn't matter to me that we share the same father. What matters most is how I feel for you." With those words, he drew her lips ever so close to his. As an encore performance to some months past, he passionately kissed her. He followed his kiss with a vow. "I will not and am not leaving you."

Her heart was won once again. "I love you too. I always have and will. But we can't do this. As much as I want to, I can't. We are siblings, you know?"

"Yes, I know. You are right. For a moment, he acted like a child whose hand was caught in the cookie jar.

Shifting gears, Carol asked, "But what about school and your scholarship?" she asked. "I don't want us to end up like our parents."

She received some reassurance. "Well," he said, "after you left the office, my parents convinced the counselor to let you remain in school. Even they saw how unfair you were treated."

"They didn't have to," she said.

"I know, but they wanted too. Besides we are in this together. They know what you sacrificed on my behalf. It's our turn to sacrifice for you."

"And what about your scholarship?" she asked.

"My parents said they will help provide for us when that time comes. Look, I promised your mother I would bring you home. I hate to say this but we need to go." There was a moment of awkwardness. Frank looked deep into Carol's soul. It was pure. "If you don't mind, can I have the ultrasound? I will give it back to you. I promise."

Carol did not hesitate. She handed it to him. "You promise to give it back?" she said smiling.

"Absolutely, we need to get going." They stood up. Out of nowhere, Frank lifted Carol off her feet. He started to carry her. "I can't afford to have you walk across the wet grass and fall. Remember, you are carrying our child."

The sun finally broke through the clouds. The winds subsided. The storm of that day had passed.

CHAPTER FIFTEEN

Frank drove Carol home. Like any true gentleman, he walked her to the door and kissed her. "I'll pick you up in the morning," he said.

He returned to his car and drove home. With Carol's ultrasound in hand, he went to his room. He sat at his bed's edge and stared at the picture for hours. He was looking at his son's heart. He wanted to know more. He needed to know more.

He went to his computer and googled the stages of pregnancy. To know what stage his son in, he compared the dates on the ultrasound to the weeks described on the web. He was captivated by what he saw. His little boy was the size of a lentil.

He laughed at his son's appearance. Zachary looked more like an alien tadpole. He had four-like fingers dangling from his head. His face resembled some type of reptile, a dinosaur perhaps. He had a tail. Though he was the size of a lentil, his spine looked more like the Rocky Mountains than vertebrae. But most importantly, he had a heartbeat.

Frank remembered telling Carol how their son was a spitting image of the father. He found the humor and chuckled out loud. "Maybe I should have done my homework before I said anything."

His mother heard Frank in his bedroom. She knocked on his door. "Honey," she asked, "is there someone with you? Dinner is almost ready, I can prepare a plate for your friend."

"No, Mom, it's just me," he responded. "Mom, come in here. There is something I want to show you."

Kelly entered the room. "What would you like to show me?"

"You got to really check this out. It is so cool," he said excitingly. He had a hard time to control or contain himself. "I can't believe it, mom. There is something far greater than me. This is it! This is proof."

His mother did not know what to say. She rubbed her son's back. "Yes, conception and birth are miraculous. We were created to create."

"Mother, there's more!" he continued. "Did you know that within two weeks, he will double in size? His hands and feet have developed. I can't wait to see what I created. I can't wait to hold him! Mom, I can't wait to hear his first word, to see his first step, and to teach him how to throw a football!"

Kelly smiled. She wasn't sure what to say. Like everyone else, she too had her doubts. She experienced firsthand the cause and effect of a teenage pregnancy. She wanted to support Frank and Carol but understood, all too well, the challenges before them. She rubbed her hand over his back. "I know sweetie! It is exciting, there is no doubt. We will have to wait and see how things pan out!"

Frank turned his head. His focus was no longer on the photos but his mother. "What in the hell does that mean?"

"Honey," she said. "So much can happen between now and the delivery date. There is the probability of a miscarriage. There is also a chance that Carol may change her mind."

"What?" he exclaimed. "Carol was right. You guys would do anything to terminate this pregnancy. She would not do that to me!"

"You have every right to feel that way," his mother explained. "But the truth is the law favors her, not you."

"That's not fair!" he shouted in anger. "The child is as much of me as it is hers. Where's the justice in that?"

"It's the law," Kelly said while now hugging her son. "It's her body; she may choose to do with the baby as she wants. There is no law protecting the rights of the father."

"And what if I choose to keep him? What rights do I have?" he said in desperation.

Kelly shook her head. "You have none, son. It's entirely her decision." She kissed the crown of his head. "Dinner is ready."

"Mom, if it's okay with you, I need some time to myself." He respectfully stated.

"I understand. I will put the leftovers in the fridge."

CHAPTER SIXTEEN

Frank remained frozen in front of his computer. He wanted to know every detail about the development of a child within the womb. He learned the next few weeks were the most critical. It was then that "Little Zach's" circulatory and neurological systems were building their bridges throughout his body. His hands and feet would have developed, and his features were more humanistic than alien-like.

His eyes grew heavy. The more he stared at the computer, the heavier they became. This time, it was Frank's time to travel back in time. His mind took him to a psalm he learned as a youth. It is Psalm 139. It reads:

O Lord, You have searched me and known me.

You know my sitting down and my rising up;
You understand my thought afar off.

You comprehend my path and my lying down,
And are acquainted with all my ways.

For there is not a word on my tongue,
But behold, O LORD, You know it altogether.

You have hedged me behind and before,
And laid Your hand upon me.

Such knowledge is too wonderful for me;
It is high, I cannot attain it.

Where can I go from Your Spirit?
Or where can I flee from Your presence?

If I ascend into heaven, You are there;
If I make my bed in hell, behold, You are there.

If I take the wings of the morning,
And dwell in the uttermost parts of the sea,

Even there Your hand shall lead me,
And Your right hand shall hold me.

If I say, "Surely the darkness shall fall on me,"
Even the night shall be light about me;

Indeed, the darkness shall not hide from You,
But the night shines as the day;
The darkness and the light are both alike to You.

For You formed my inward parts;
You covered me in my mother's womb.

I will praise You, for I am fearfully
and wonderfully made;

Marvelous are Your works,
And that my soul knows very well.

My frame was not hidden from You,
When I was made in secret,

And skillfully wrought in the
lowest parts of the earth.

Your eyes saw my substance, being yet unformed.
And in Your book they all were written,
The days fashioned for me,
When as yet there were none of them.

How precious also are Your thoughts to me, O God!
How great is the sum of them!
(Psalm 139:1-17; NKJV)

God's word had a profound effect. Though he slept, he was comforted. His fears, doubts, and concerns about his child were quickly dismissed. He had a peace that passed all understanding. He knew God was with him. Regardless of how his child was conceived, he knew that God had a place and a plan for his child.

Before he knew it, his state of tranquility was abruptly interrupted. The morning had sprung. There he sat with the computer now staring at him. The last thing he remembered was researching the dynamics of life. With the early morning sun peeking through his window and his mother banging on his door, he quickly glanced at his clock. "Shit!" he yelled. "Carol!"

"Is everything okay?" his mother asked.

"Yes Mom, everything is fine," he blurted out. Hastily, he got dressed, combed his hair and brushed his teeth. He ran to his room. He grabbed the ultrasound from his desk and then rushed to the door as if running to the goal line. Frank broke through the furniture without breaking any. He was halfway through the threshold when he heard his mother ask, "what's your hurry? Are you meeting your friends?"

With his back to his mother, his answer was muffled. "I promised to drive Carol to school!"

Kelly shook her head and shrugged her shoulders. "Okay," she thought. With her eyebrows raised, she whispered, "Please drive safely."

CHAPTER SEVENTEEN

Frank hurried to Carol's. He found her waiting on the porch. He pulled into the driveway. She got in his car. He decided to talk with Carol before they went to school. He drove to a vacant parking lot. Her heart filled with excitement and uncertainty.

Frank turned his eyes right and stared into hers. "Good morning," he said. "I apologize for my tardiness. I was up late last night…" Carol did not give him a chance to finish his thoughts. Her curiosity got the best of her.

"What were you doing?" she asked.

He smiled. His sea-blue eyes caught her off-guard. They radiated the depth of his sincerity. "I studied."

Carol cocked her head back. She gave him a bewildered look. "What did you study?"

"I looked into our baby's development! I took the ultrasound and compared it to photos I found on the internet. I was amazed. I never knew or understood everything involved." He stopped. His enthusiasm was quickly drowned by his tears. He sobbed uncontrollably. He placed both hands on her cheeks. "We can't abort our child! I beg you."

She slapped his arm. "Oh, quit your crying, silly. I am not aborting our child."

He used his sleeve to wipe his eyes and then his nose. "Do you promise? I need you to promise me. I want to be our child's father. We can make it work, I know we can."

"I know!" she confidently answered. The same hand she used to slap him, she also used to run her thumb across his tear-soaked cheek. "If it is a promise you want, then it is a promise I will give you." Like a mother kissing her child, she skillfully and softly kissed his cheek. She placed her forehead against his. "We are in this together."

"Yes, yes we are," he said. "I am not going anywhere." As earlier, he did everything to make himself presentable. He wiped his face, straightened his hair, and regained his composure. "Oh, before I forget, here is the ultrasound of our son."

"Thank you," she softly spoke. "Can we go to school now?"

He put his car in gear, and said: "As you wish." The new season started to make its appearance. A heavy snow started to fall. The trees welcomed the snow to paint their barren limbs. Frank demonstrated his experience behind the wheel. He drove with confidence. He conquered the snow-covered roads.

CHAPTER EIGHTEEN

Frank pulled into his personal parking spot. It was close to the school. Outside of being a senior, he was a star quarterback. He earned that spot. He was soon to learn that his standing in school was more of a privilege than a right. He was also soon to learn about another flurry soon to take place. This time, the advancing front came from the student body. It was a front he did not see coming. It was a front he did not know how to control. It was a front he could not conquer.

It was felt immediately. Frank and Carol barely entered the school when they felt eyes beating on them. A fellow student overheard the conversation that took place in the counselor's office. Like any juicy story, he did not hesitate to light the match. He told a friend, who told another friend…The rumor mill started. Word ran rampant. It was out of control. By days end, everyone knew of their incestuous relationship. Though no one verbalized it, Frank and Carol felt the tension amongst their friends.

Side by side, they walked. They tried to maintain some sense of pride and dignity. It was not their fault. Had they known about their parents, they would not be in this predicament. Sadly, there is a difference between pride and dignity. It was Frank's pride that would be challenged. In the process of protecting it, he would lose his dignity.

He walked Carol to her locker when someone shouted, "How does it feel to knock-up your sister? Man, you are sick!" Immediately, Frank turned his attention in the direction of the person shouting. Unbelievably, it was his best friend Scott. Frank couldn't believe it. He and Scott were like brothers. They relied on one another, especially on the football field. Like Frank, Scott was granted a scholarship. There was one difference between them. Scott was heading to an Ivy League Team.

Years of friendship ended with an exchange of flurries. Frank made the first move. There was no way he would allow someone to diminish his character, let alone Carol's. He bull-rushed Scott. He slammed his longtime friend against the lockers. It stunned Scott. He fell to the floor dazed. Frank wasted no time. He jumped on his opponent, where he relentlessly beat him. Blood splattered across the lockers and the walls.

Frank's screams echoed off the block walls. "You are a son of a bitch," he blurted. "I thought we were friends. How dare you judge me without knowing the facts?" With each passing statement, Frank instilled another blow. He rendered Scott speechless and helpless.

Of all people to separate the two men, it was the counselor. He did not hesitate to run down the hall, break through the circle that encapsulated the two, and pull Frank off of Scott. "That's enough," he declared. He directed his attention to Frank. "Young man, I need you in my office now!" He pointed to two fellow football players. His frustration was evident. "I can't believe you two didn't stop this! You are teammates. Is that how you play on the field? You guys should be watching out for one another." He caught his breath and gave an order. "Help him to his feet, and take him to the nurse's station."

Frank stood motionless. The reality of the situation set in. He committed a crime. It was a crime against his best friend. The counselor was in no mood for sympathy. He grabbed Frank by his shoulder and jerked him in the direction of the school office.

No longer did the counselor act as dumb as he looked. Students saw a different side of him. He was strong and, when needed, he was not to be reckoned with. Since Frank remained spellbound by his actions, the counselor helped him. With both hands, he pushed

Frank down the hallway. "When I say move boy, I mean move. Don't stand there with your thumb up your ass. Get going."

Carol did not know how to react. Frank was protecting her honor, as well as his. The counselor must have known. He heard everything. "It is not our fault!" she thought. She prayed for leniency, but that was not in the forecast.

Before the first bell rang, Frank lost his privileges. In time, he would lose everything.

CHAPTER NINETEEN

Frank and the counselor marched into the office. Frank was jolted when he heard the door slam behind him. The counselor wasted no time in reading the riot act. "Sit down!" he shouted. Frank buried his head in his hands. The adrenaline that fueled the fire was no longer present. His raw emotions now took the helm. His only recourse to rectify the two extremes was to cry.

"What in the hell was that all about?" the counselor blurted.

"I couldn't let him get away with it?" Frank cried out. He lifted his head. Snot dangled from his nose. It started to mix with the salty water that flowed down his cheeks.

The counselor threw a box of Kleenex at him. "Here, wipe your face. I can't stand to see mucous dripping from someone's nose. So, tell me, young man, what did Scott do that you couldn't let him get away with?"

"It's not what did. It's what he said. He called me and Carol sick."

The counselor leaned the hollow of his back against his desk. He crossed his arms and shook his head in disgust. "You have to be joking. That's it. Did you beat the shit out of your best friend because of that? Give me a break! How did you expect your friends to react?"

"What do you expect of me?" Frank blurted.

"I expected you to be the leader. I expected to be bigger than that. I expected you to walk away." the counselor replied. "Right now, I have two options. I can expel you or suspend you. It's your choice."

"What about my scholarship?"

What about it?" the counselor asked.

"Will I lose it?" Frank demanded to know.

"Young man," the counselor responded. "You should have thought about that before you went ballistic. To answer your question, if I were you, I would not be expecting a phone call soon."

Frank popped tall from his chair. "You mean I lost it."

"Is that the only thing you are worried about? "I am afraid you did. By law, I have to report this incident to the college. It will be on your record." The counselor was to point. "So, returning to my question. Which would you rather have? Would you rather be suspended or expelled? It's your choice."

"This is not fair! Scott started it! Why must I be the only one to suffer?"

The counselor somewhat chuckled. "I believe I heard that same question yesterday. Do you remember? It's called consequences. A scholarship is not the only thing you need to worry about. Because of the brutality of your actions, I have no choice but to file a police report. My hands are tied. If I don't report it to the authorities, Scott's parents have every right to."

Frank shook his head. He couldn't believe this was happening. He protected his and Carol's pride. In the process, his lost his dignity.

"Let's get back to the original question. Do you want to be expelled or suspended?"

"At this point, does it really matter?" Frank asked with his head looking at the floor.

"Believe it or not, it does," the counselor said. "Expulsion would be the easy route. You would no longer face your peers. You can go about your business as if nothing ever happened: unless charges are pressed. Suspension, young man, requires you to face the challenge before you, and move on."

"How am I supposed to explain this to my parents?" Frank added.

"Based on our conversation yesterday, I have a hunch they will perfectly understand. "Look," the counselor went on to explain. "Character, young man, is not defined by what you did. It is defined by what you do to change it. You have your whole life ahead of you. I encourage you to own up to what happened and move forward. Let the chips fall where they may. Take the suspension. Jeopardizing your scholarship does not prevent you from attending college."

Disappointed in what he did, Frank took the counselor's advice. He opted for the suspension. Christmas break was within a week. By the time he returned to school, it would be a new year. He was concerned about Scott. He prayed Scott would forgive him and like the New Year, they could start anew.

CHAPTER TWENTY

Frank was at a loss. He was beside himself. He left the office and exited the school. He approached his car perched in its privileged position. It was buried in four inches of snow. Before he opened his driver's side door, he turned to look at his school. It was barely visible. It was blinded by steadily fallen snow. For Frank, it was symbolic. It was a sign. Everything he worked for and aspired to be was no longer in sight.

He cleared the snow off his car. He backed up only to see the spot he once claimed. It was a reminder of what was to be. Now it lay barren. In time, the spot he prized would be like everything around. It would be covered.

He slowly drove home. Many times he thought about crashing his car into a telephone pole. "At least there would be peace in death," he would say out loud. Yet, there were two things that came to mind: his dream and the counselor's words, "Character, young man, is not defined in what you did but by what you do to change it."

He knew God had plans for him as his son and he knew his counselor was right. Driving into some foreign object would prove nothing, but add misery to the others. He pounded his hands against his steering wheel and shouted, "That's not who I am! It's not what I'm about!"

His pep talk rekindled his passion to succeed. He did not need a scholarship to validate his athleticism. He could attend college without suiting up. He did not have to terminate his life. He was responsible for giving life. The more he mediated on these things, the stronger he became in mind and spirit.

By that time he reached his driveway, his mind was made up. He will brush the dust from his knees, pick himself up, and press forward. In the end, he would persevere.

He went to his room. He returned to his computer. Its screen was blank. He touched the mouse. The image picked up where it left off some hours before. It pictured the development of a child within the womb. His fascination intensified. He wanted to finish what he started. He continued to study the various stages.

His time was interrupted when someone knocked on the door. "Who could that be?" he thought. He did everything to brush off the distraction, but the more he ignored it the more the banging continued. "Shit!" he yelled. "Can't I be alone?"

Finally, he left his seat and answered the door. It was Carol. "What are you doing here?" he shouted with excitement.

"School ended early because of the weather." She hesitated and then gave him a cold look. "Well," she said, "are you going to stand there or are you going to invite me in? I am freezing."

"Absolutely, please come in." Frank countered. "Would you like a towel or something warm to drink?" he asked.

"Something warm to drink would be nice," she responded. It was her first time in Frank's home. Everything was extravagant. Everything was in its place. She thought about all the possibilities Frank's family could provide for her "Little Zach."

Frank re-entered the foyer. "Here is some hot tea. I was going to make you coffee, but that's not good for our child." He handed her the cup. His curiosity got the best of him. "By the way, how did you get here?"

With her gloves already removed, she smacked his arm. "Don't be silly, silly," she said smiling. "I walked."

"Are you crazy? That's a three-mile hike in the snow. And let's not forget, you are pregnant."

Franks sincerity showed. She knew he cared. "I know, but I thought you could use a friend after this morning."

"Yeah," he sighed. "I thought yesterday was crazy. This morning took the cake. I am not sure how to explain it to my parents."

"He started it. Had he not said anything, you would not have done what you did."

"No, the counselor was right. I should have and could have walked away," Frank openly admitted. "My emotions got the best of me. It is one thing to learn that the girl you love is with child, it is another thing to find out she is your own flesh and blood. Not to mention, I played like shit last Saturday. I threw four interceptions. If that did not cost me a scholarship, this morning surely did."

Frank was on the verge of an emotional breakdown. He did everything to contain himself. Carol set her tea on a nearby table, extended her arms and pulled Frank to her. There she embraced him. She used her right hand to run her fingers through his hair.

"It's okay. You are allowed to be human. I wouldn't want you any other way," she said in a nurturing voice. "This morning you defended me. You shielded me from the others. I don't think anyone will make that mistake again, especially Scott."

"Scott," Frank whispered. "Is he okay?"

"I was afraid you might ask." Carol's tone changed. She became extremely nervous. She released her hold on him. She softly looked into his eyes. "Do you really want to know?"

"Yes, I need to know." Frank was apprehensive. He was very much afraid. He had every reason to be. He feared the worst. He would be arrested for assaulting his friend.

Carol remained silent. She refused to answer his question. Frank patiently waited. Behind them was a grandfather clock. He could each ticking second. Its sound became stronger with each passing second. Frank's apprehension rose in direct proportion with each tick of the clock. His heart started to race and he started to sweat.

In desperation, he pleaded with Carol. "Please tell me. How is Scott?"

"Listen, Frank," she tried to explain. "I don't see how you will benefit. You are already anxious as it is."

Frank was exhausted. He wanted it to be over. "Maybe so," he said, but I do need to own up for what I caused.

Despite her wishes, Carol did as Frank requested. She shared Scott's condition. "After you left, his mother was called. I saw her walking with Scott down the hall. Scott had an ice bag over his nose. His eyes were bruised and his face was severely lacerated. I overheard someone say he required medical attention. According to the school nurse, you broke his nose and the lacerations required stitches."

"Is there anything else I should know," Frank asked. He trembled as he waited to hear her answer.

"They are afraid that Scott suffered a head injury. How serious it is, no one knows. Their concern stems from his head slamming against the lockers and floor. I saw his mother's face as they passed me. She was furious. Apparently, she threatened to file charges against the assailant and legal litigation on the school."

Kelly, Frank's mother, happened to come home early. Since she served on the school board, she caught wind of her son's suspension and what prompted it. She also learned about Scott's condition as well as his mother's threat to sue the person responsible.

She tried to stay composed, but her emotions got the best of her. When she first saw Frank and Carol standing in her foyer, her composure flew out the door. Looking directly at Carol, she blatantly asked Carol, "May I ask what you are doing in my house? Haven't you created enough chaos for everyone?"

Frank came to Carol's defense. "Mom, she had nothing to do with this morning. It was my choice, not hers."

"I appreciate your honesty and your willingness to protect this young lady. I believe it is best that neither of you sees nor talk to one another. Anything from this point on will be subject to scrutiny and scandal. That's the last thing we need." She stopped. She saw the pain in their eyes. "Frank, I believe it best you drive Carol home. The police will here soon. Scott's mother is pressing charges against you. I can't blame her. I don't blame her. You seriously injured her son."

Frank and Carol looked toward one another in disbelief. This is not what they asked for or wished. They did not argue with Kelly. Instead, they obliged to her request.

CHAPTER TWENTY-ONE

Frank drove Carol home. There was not much to say. Though they never said it, they thought it. "Is this what we have to look forward to? How will our decision affect Zachary?" They didn't want to think about it. They tried to block it from their young minds, but they couldn't.

The snow continued its fall from the heavens. Driving, like their lives, became difficult. Frank did not have the control over the road as he did earlier. Only God knew the course he would soon travel. Slowly, he pulled into Carol's driveway. He looked at her. There were so many things he wanted to say, but couldn't. He wanted to kiss her, but couldn't.

His heart broke knowing they would never be the same. She was with child. The child was his. Yes, he was conceived out of love. But that love was never meant to be. While the thought of an abortion came to mind, it was not an option. He recalled the dream he had. The conditions and circumstances of conception were not his son's fault.

Carol distracted Frank's train of thought when she handed him the ultrasound. "Here, I want you to have this. It is a reminder of the promise that awaits us. I don't want you to lose hope. I made a promise. I will keep it."

Frank stared at the blur. He smiled. The hope he lost, he regained. "That's our baby," he said. The clouds that once blocked the sun separated. In turn, he saw a ray of sun beat on his windshield. Like the clouds above, his anxiety subsided.

The clouds continued to part when Carol gasped. She held her stomach. What was considered a flutter became a kick. "Frank!" she shouted. "Our son is telling us something. I felt him. Here touch."

Frank leaned over. He placed his hand on Carol's abdomen. "Little Zach" made his existence know. He did as Carol said. He kicked. Frank's blue eyes lit up. He was deemed speechless. Whereas the ultrasound showed Zachary's existence, his little foot against his mother's womb proved it. He was indeed a father.

He and Carol exchanged hugs. They resisted the temptation to take their feelings any further. Zachary's existence gave Frank the strength to face whatever awaited him. Sure he lost his standing among his peers and even a scholarship, but the thought of a son took precedence.

Through Zachary, Frank would eradicate the wrongs of his father. For years, he often wondered what he did so terribly wrong that his father abstained from forming anything that resembled a relationship. No matter how hard Frank tried to prove himself, it was never enough. His father was void of love and was vacant for much of Frank's life. Now, Frank understood. It all made sense. He was not Frank's father. Frank was nothing more than a complimentary gift. It was Kelly his father sought. Yet, in the end, his father lost. Kelly's heart belonged to another.

He made a vow never to let that happen between him and Zachary. He would do everything and anything for "Little Zach." He would do for his son what his father never did for him. He would love his son to no end.

Had he known what was waiting for him, he may have thought differently. A police car was parked in front of his house. It caught him off-guard. Sure his mother forewarned him. He completely forgot. The reality of the situation did not sink in until he saw that reality sitting on his street. Yes, he committed a crime. Of all things, he assaulted a lifelong friend.

Though a part of him did not want to, he was ready to own up for what he did. He pulled into the driveway. He did not have time to get out of his vehicle. Two police officers approached him from the rear. With guns drawn, they ordered him out of the car.

He was reluctant. "Is this really necessary?" he shouted from his window.

"Get out of the car!" on officer ordered, with your hands in the air."

"You got to be shitting me," he mumbled. He exited the car with both hands in the air. In his right hand was the ultrasound. He tried to tuck it in his front pocket but to no avail. Before he knew it, his hands were behind his back and he was cuffed.

One of the officers' saw the film in his hand. Hurriedly, he snatched it from Frank's grip. The ultrasound was torn in two. Frank's reluctance turned into resistance. He fought to get the officer's away from him. "I want my picture back," he demanded.

"Son," the officer said, "you are in no position to bargain. Either you settle down or we have no choice but to settle you down. It's up to you."

"I want my picture back!" Frank shouted. "It's a picture of my unborn son. Give it to me and I will surrender peacefully."

The officer glanced at the photo. "This!" he laughed. "This is nothing! Boy, I would think twice if I were you."

"It's nothing to you, but he's everything to me. Please give me what I asked for. I promise to cooperate.

The officer tucked the snapshot in Frank's shirt pocket. "Here it is Romeo," he chided. "If it's going to shut you up, I am all for it. Now, get your sorry ass in the car. You are under arrest for aggravated assault. You have the right…."

He looked at his house. He saw his mother and father watching from the window. He was shocked by what he saw. Neither one made any attempt to come outside. Instead, his mother clasped her hands over her mouth, while his father's rested his hands on his waist. Both parents shook their heads, but for different reasons. His mother showed sympathy and his father expressed shame.

In exchange, Frank reciprocated his parents' actions. He shook his head. The police placed him in the squad car. He couldn't believe this was happening to him. A few days ago, people looked up to him.

They loved him. He came to personify the All-American student. Now, he was treated like a criminal. His rights and privileges were stripped. His dignity was gone. And the freedoms he once enjoyed were no longer.

He felt alone. He felt abandoned. The officers did not help. They poked fun at his performance on the field. "So," the officer said, "It appears you know how to throw your balls around except on the football field. You threw four interceptions…how does that make you feel?"

Frank did not respond. He was in enough trouble. "Common son," the officer countered, "did you forget how to talk? Oh let me guess, you are more concerned about your baby boy than your community. Well boy, let me ask you this: what makes you believe it's yours. You know I am talking about your mother. She's nothing more than a tramp. Everyone knows it. She'd sneak by your girlfriend's house and bang her father." The officer turned his hand to face Frank. He laughed. "It must run in the family don't you think?"

Frank refused to offer a rebuttal. Instead, he held his head down and prayed.

"What's the matter," the officer asked, "a cat has your tongue? Don't you worry; the fun has yet to begin. Wait till we get to the station," the officer said. "I hope you like the accommodations we have prepared for you."

CHAPTER TWENTY-TWO

Like Frank, Carol would find herself confined. She sat in her bedroom and daydreamed. Her mind floated from one scene to the next. She envisioned the birth of her son. The thought of holding her son for the first time made her smile. She wondered who he would favor most, her or Frank. In either case, the baby was destined to be good-looking.

She was comforted to think of her son's unconditional love. He would not judge her for what she did or didn't do. His concerns would primarily be focused on her. She was, of course, the lifeline to his life. To experience the love a mother has for a child and a child for his mother was unfathomable.

Her time alone was interrupted. Maria heard about the fight. She left work early. In her mind, "Enough was enough! This had to end." She burst through Carol's bedroom door. She was flabbergasted. Carol was on her back. She was staring literally into nowhere.

"How long are you going keep this shit up?" she screamed. "Don't you think enough people have suffered because of your decision? End this now, before it gets out of hand!"

Carol's trance was broken. She rolled over and faced mother. "What are you talking about? Frank wants this baby as much as I do."

"That's bullshit," Maria snorted. "I thought the same thing when I carried you. If anyone should know the hardships that follow, it should be me!"

Carol was oblivious to her mother's speech. "Mother, what are you talking about?"

"I am talking about me and your father," Maria shouted. "We convinced ourselves that we could handle the pressure. You witnessed firsthand how that worked out. Your father not only continued his relationship with the other woman, but he ended his life as well. I refuse to let you follow in our footsteps."

"Mom," Carol shouted, "This is different! Frank would never do that to me."

"You are wrong. You are dead wrong," Maria countered. "Frank is in jail. He has lost everything because of you.

Carol refused to listen to her mother. Things between her and Frank were different. They loved one another. It was out their love "Little Zach" was conceived.

Maria had no choice but to render her sentence. She desperately tried to make her daughter understand. Carol would have nothing to do with it. She forced her mother's hand. "I understand," she said. Her heart was torn. She cried one too many times over this affair. "That's fine. This evening I want you to pack your personal belongings."

Carol was dumbfounded. She was not sure where her mother was going with this. "For what?" she asked half-heartedly. "Let me guess, you are sending me to a boarding house for teenage mothers."

Much to Maria's dismay, she answered Carol. With tear-soaked eyes, she affirmed her intentions. "Get your things in order: you left me with no other choice."

CHAPTER TWENTY-THREE

Frank's evening in the county lockup was more than he could handle. He did not like being stripped search. He did not like being pushed around by the guards. He did not like being treated like a criminal. He did not like his cell. And he did not like his cellmates.

His world crashed in on him. Everything he gained, he lost. His life represented his three cellmates. It was confined. It was complicated. In his eyes, it was over. He couldn't believe it. Had he just walked away, he would not be in this predicament. His only comfort was the ultrasound he still carried. But even that created conflict.

He did not converse with the others in his cell. He sat silent. He stared at the two pieces of paper. They represented the cause of his incarceration. He tried to convince himself that it was a noble cause. As before, he had his doubts.

Those doubts were confirmed when one of the cellmates questioned him. "What are looking at boy?"

Frank attempted to stand tall and on his own. "It's not your concern. You mind your own business, and I will mind mine."

Another cellmate chimed in. He recognized Frank. "Hey," he asked, "aren't you the star quarterback for the high school? What did you do, run a stop sign?"

"What is to you?" Frank shot back.

Frank remained fixated on the ultrasound. The first cellmate walked up to Frank and snatched the pictures from his hand. "Well, look here! It seems that our star quarterback is soon to be a daddy!" He emphasized his enthusiasm by smacking Frank in the head. "No wonder you threw for four interceptions last week. Your head was somewhere else. Is that right boy?"

"Shut up!" Frank demanded. "You don't know what you are talking about."

"Is that so? Well, we will see about that." The cellmate looked at the other two men locked up. "Gentlemen," he calmly said, "it seems our friend likes to screw around. I think we should screw with him a bit. What you do guys say?"

Both men stood up. "Sounds like a fine plan to me!" The one shouted.

"Me too," the other countered.

Before Frank knew it, the three men surrounded him. The leader smiled and said, "Boy, you can make this easy on yourself, or you can make it hard. It's up to you!"

Frank rose from his seated position. The three men underestimated Frank's size. He was considerably taller than his counterparts. He was also considerably in better shape. He looked down on his opposition. "Men!" he said as he stared each man in the eyes. "I am afraid I must decline the invitation. I would suggest you back up and off or bring it on."

The ringleader walked toward Frank. "Now are you a feisty son-of-a-bitch. "Look, boy, I don't care how big you are or how bad you think you are. There is three of us and one of you."

The star athlete found humor in what was happening. He was used to being hit and tackled. The men refused to lose their ground. Frank chuckled.

"You don't see me laughing. We are going to have your ass," the leader shouted.

"We will have to see," Frank said confidently. He did not allow the cellmates to make the first move. He knew better. He clenched his fist and struck the man in front of him. He hit him with such force; the man flew off his feet. He smacked against the cell wall five feet behind him. In the process, he lost his two front teeth.

He spit his blood at Frank. "Well now, that changes things," he said.

Frank walked to him. He grabbed his son's ultrasound from the man's hand. "It would be in your best interests to stay right where you are!" Frank shouted while pointing his finger at the man's face. He stood up and turned to the other two men. "Who wants to be next?" he demanded to know. With that, both men withdrew.

Thankfully, the guard saw the altercation on camera. He rushed to the cell. He opened the door and pointed to Frank. "Young man," he said laughing, "someone has posted your bail."

The guard led Frank to a changing room. He handed Frank his clothes. They were still stained with Scott's blood. "Today must be your lucky day young man," the guard said. "Get changed," He ordered. He then asked, "Have you ever thought about boxing?"

Frank raised his eyebrows. That was a strange question, he thought. "Why do you ask?"

"From what I saw on the camera and what I heard you did to your friend, you do have one hell of a punch," the guard replied as he unlocked the changing room door. "You have five minutes. I will be waiting."

The guard did not have to repeat the order. Frank burst through the doors that lead him to freedom. He immediately took off his prison garb and changed into his civilian clothes. He examined the blood splatter and then stared at the ultrasound. "Son," he whispered, "I sure pray you are worth this." He took the two pieces of paper and returned them to his front pocket.

CHAPTER TWENTY-FOUR

The guard escorted Frank through the halls. They walked up a flight of steps and with one swipe of the guard's card, Frank was a free man. His excited was interrupted when he saw Carol's mother, Maria standing near.

His immediate thought was, "What is she doing here?"

He did not have time to ask the question, she answered it before he asked it aloud. "Young man, you are coming with me," she politely said. For a moment, she thought Frank was a marble statue. He stood frozen in time. "Well, are you coming or not?"

He thought about his alternatives. Would he rather remain caged with his three amigos or experience the freedom that awaited him? He chose the latter. Quietly, he followed Maria outside. Slowly they walked to her car. The snow showers had ceased. The roads were smooth sailing. He hoped this was a sign. Had he known what he was signing onto, he would have thought differently.

"I will drive you home," she said, "on a few conditions."

"What's that?" Frank queried.

"I want you to listen to everything I have to say. I want you to agree with everything I have to say," she explained. Her voice was crisp. It was curt. "The moment you disagree, I will not hesitate to put your ass back where it belongs."

His options were limited. "I can't agree to anything unless I understand what I am agreeing too," he said.

"We will discuss that on your way home," she sternly said. "Get in the car, or I will not hesitate to send you from whence you came."

Frank did as instructed. He took the passenger's seat. He sat still. He sat silent. He listened.

Maria was now in the driver's seat. She was in control. She opted to take her time. She waited until she finally broke the silence. She cleared her throat before she spoke. "As you know, I bailed you out. In some ways, I hold the keys to your future. You either abide by my rules, or I will throw your ass back in jail."

"I heard you the first time," Frank said anxiously. "What do you want from me?"

"I am glad you asked. I want you to stay away from my daughter. You two have no business together. Too many people have been hurt. It ends tonight."

"With all due respect," Frank countered, "she is pregnant with my child."

Maria showed a side she seldom shared. She was sympathetic. "I know. I am partially to blame for this mess. Please remember, things are a little more complicated with you two. You both share the same father. You are siblings."

"Yes, ma'am," Frank said apologetically, "I am fully aware of that fact. It was not our fault. We didn't know."

"I understand. Believe me, I understand. However, I am concerned about Carol as much as I am you. Neither one of you deserves this. You have a bright future ahead of you. I don't want to see you ruin it."

Frank could not control himself. He started to cry. "I'm sorry, but from what I understand, my future does not seem as promising as it did twelve hours ago."

"That's not true." Maria went on to explain. "I spoke with Scott's parents this afternoon. They will not press charges against you. Their only request is you pay restitution for the medical expenses they accrued. If you do, there will be no public record of this morning's mishap."

"And where does Carol fit into all of this?" Frank asked.

"You let me worry about her," Maria clearly stated. "From this point on, you are to abstain from any contact with her."

"And if I don't?" Frank asked.

"I will press charges against you," Maria sternly replied. Frank knew she meant business. She made no bones about it. "You see, while I was posting your bail, I also filed a restraining order against you. If you come anywhere near her, I will have you arrested. If you call her, I will have you arrested. If you even think about her, I will have you arrested. Do I make myself clear, young man?"

"Is Carol okay with this?" Frank questioned. He was afraid of the answer he received. His worst fears came to fruition. He and Carol would be separated. In the end, Maria would have the final say.

"She doesn't know. It's best that she doesn't," Maria fired back. "Besides, I instructed her to pack her personal belongings. She will be leaving town first thing in the morning."

"Where are you sending her?" Frank demanded to know.

"That is not you concern, young man," Maria responded without hesitation. "I need you to focus on your future. Let me take care of Carol."

Frank shook his head. He couldn't shake the feeling. He would never see Carol or their child. "I don't think I necessarily appreciate where this is leading"

"Let me offer you some advice," Maria firmly said. "If I were you, I would stop thinking. It will get you in a world of trouble. Don't stare a gifted horse in the mouth," she advised. "It's not too late. You have been given a second chance to make something of yourself. Don't blow it."

CHAPTER TWENTY-FIVE

Carol did not sleep. She feared what her mother would do. She thought about packing her things and running away. She had nowhere to go. The only person who cared was Lucy. That option was null and void. Lucy was reeling the consequences from punching Frank. The weather outside was too wet and cold for her to walk. Besides, it was dark. Her primary concern was for "Little Zach." She needed to protect him, despite the costs. She wanted to see him. She wanted her ultrasound back. At least that was tangible. It was something for her to hold onto.

Morning came sooner than expected. Carol was sitting in her chair. She stared out the window. There were children outside. They were waiting for their bus. She remembered the time when she was that age. Everything then seemed so innocent. Her only worry back then was the time she went to bed. She remembered her father tucking her in. He would kiss her on the forehead and whisper, "Good night princess, Daddy loves you." She would close her eyes only to hear the door softly close.

She started to cry. She missed her father. She needed her father. She whispered, "I love you too Daddy." She recalled the last time she saw him. He was on the bathroom floor and blood spewed the shower stall. She was overcome by hopelessness. She felt helpless to save him. A part of her life ended that day. She looked toward the heavens and screamed, "Why Daddy! Why did you leave me! Talk to me: dammit Daddy, your little princess is talking to you. Her heart was laced with guilt. "I never had the chance to say goodbye or how much I loved you. If I did, maybe you would still be here today. Daddy, Please, I beg you to come home!"

Her pleas fell on deaf ears. Her father never answered. He never came. He never comforted her. He would never return home. "What was I thinking?" Reminding herself, she said "He's dead! He's dead! He's dead!"

She bowed her head. She held her belly. She turned her attention to her "Little Zach." "I will never do that to you," she said so tenderly. She felt one tear as it fell from her cheek. "I will never leave you. You will always be loved."

Maria happened to march in while Carol spoke to Zach. "I sure hope so. He's going to need it," she snapped. "Did you pack your belongings?"

"No, I did not," Carol shot back. "I am not going anywhere with you."

Maria glared. If looks could kill, Carol would be dead. "Yes, yes you are. Remember, you asked for this."

Carol jumped from her seat. She glared back. She pointed her finger to make a point. "How did I ask for this mother? You act like I screwed the whole school. Well, I didn't. Frank was my first. I'm not to blame that he's my brother."

"Don't look at me! I am not his father. If you want to point your finger then aim at your father. He's the one who couldn't keep his pants up!" Maria flung her arms in the air. "I'm done arguing with you. You better be ready in five minutes."

"Where are you taking me?" Carol shouted.

"You are going to live with your Aunt Alice!"

"She lives out of state!" Carol argued. "That's not fair. What about Frank?"

Maria was halfway down the hall when she yelled out, "What about him?"

Carol grabbed a suitcase from her closet. She was livid. She struggled to make sense of everything. There was no sense to be made. There was one resolution. There was one absolute. She was keeping her baby. She flung whatever clothes could fit into her case. She grabbed her undergarments and toiletries. "I hope this makes that bitch of mother happy." She mumbled. "Aunt Alice's can't be any worse than this."

She started out her door when turned back. There on her bed was a white teddy bear. Her father won it at an amusement park. It meant the world to her at one time. She never went to bed without him. She set her case down. She approached the bear as a parent approaches a baby. She picked him up. She tucked him and kissed him on the forehead. She whispered in his furry ear, "I love you, Daddy."

CHAPTER TWENTY-SIX

Maria waited in the car. She looked at her watch. "What is taking her so long? We need to get going," she thought. She was about to step out of the car when she saw Carol walk out. "It's about damn time she listened." Maria shook her head. She gave her daughter a cold and condescending stare.

Carol put her suitcase in the backseat. She got in the front seat. Their conversation picked up where it left off. "What was that look? I thought you would happy to finally get rid of me and my problem." Carol spouted.

"Don't give me that shit! Maria barked back. "I am not in the mood."

"And what makes you think that I am. Do you think I am happy about everything? Well, mother, I am not. As a matter of fact, I am disappointed. Yes, disappointed. Apparently, what I feel and how I feel isn't important. At least Dad cared." Carol said.

"Oh my gosh, am I going to have to listen to this crap for the next two hours?" Maria snarled. "Can't you wait till we leave the driveway before you start ranting and raving about how I failed as your mother?"

Carol respected her mother's request. She rested her hands on her thighs. She sat silent. Since the roads wore a fresh coat of snow, she did not want to distract her mother. She could ill afford to be involved in an accident. She didn't want to be blamed for something else. Besides, she was with child.

She hoped their time together would be more beneficial than a burden. She recognized bridges were burned between them. She so desperately wanted to rebuild them. She waited for a good time to extinguish the flames. She waited for the right time to reconstruct what was lost.

She seized her opportunity when they approached a place they frequented in the past. It was an old church. It was well hidden from the road. Most people were oblivious to its existence. At one time, it was thriving. It was a pillar of the community. However, it suffered several losses. The congregation refused to catch up to the times. It's preaching and practices were considered antiquated by most people. So too were the congregants. People started to die off without having a future generation to carry on its legacy. Eventually, it was forced to close its doors.

Sadly, this old-time church was constructed on the banks of a lake. The panoramic view it painted was beyond description. In the summer, people were amazed by its reflection in the waves ripples. In the autumn leaves announce God's artistic touch. The snow echoed the power of redemption, and the spring brought forth rejuvenation.

Carol and her family had fond memories of this now abandoned church. Carol was dedicated there. She accepted Christ there. She was baptized there. She dreamt that one day she would walk down the aisle there. Those dreams were shattered when the church had no choice but to close its doors.

"Mom," she fondly asked, "do you think we can stop by our old church?"

Maria was stunned. She did not know what to say. The exit was quickly advancing. By all appearances, Maria had no intentions of honoring Carol's petition. Suddenly, she jerked the car to the ramp. The car slid across the highway. It nearly rammed against a guardrail. "I don't know why I am doing this, but if it's important to you, then it's important to me."

"Thank you," Carol said.

Maria regained control and drove slowly around the lake. The majestic view captured her spirit. She saw two deer prancing across the ice-covered water. One was female, the other was male. They were playing and preparing the course God created for them. Something dawned on Maria. Her daughter did what was only natural. She followed her maternal instincts and intuition.

The closer they came to the church, the more difficult it was to drive. Snowdrifts swept across the open fields. The road they traveled was barely recognizable and so too was the church. Years of neglect paid its toll on the old structure. Its windows were broken, boarded up, or both. The steeple that once towered over the landscape had toppled. Parts of the roof had collapsed. The white siding that once illuminated the outside structure was now covered with soot. And the stained glass windows, that bore the impressions of their faith, had been shattered.

Maria went as far as her car would permit. She questioned her ability to maneuver her way back to the main road. Carol opened the door. She started to get out when Maria interrupted her progress. "Honey, I don't want you to go in there."

"I have to mother," she quietly responded. "I don't know why, but I am being drawn to it."

"What are you hoping to find? This church has nothing to offer you. It's dead"

Carol's words were from the Spirit encouraging her to break through all barriers. "You would think, but I am learning that even in death, there is life. I must go." She stopped. She thought. She said, "You want to know what I am looking for? I am looking peace."

She proceeded to push her way to the church. It was difficult, especially for a pregnant woman. She approached the front entrance. The steps leading to the entrance were covered with the snow. She was not sure of their true condition. She assumed they were like much of this old-time church: that is, broken. She carefully took each step up the steps. She came to the front doors. Though boarded at one time, they freely blew open in the mid-morning breeze.

She entered the sanctuary. She was saddened to see it in its current condition. The plaster that covered the cathedral ceiling had collapsed. Chunks now plastered the pews and the floors. She looked up to the rafters where she saw some bird's nesting. She smiled to know this place of worship was very much alive. It was occupied by God's creation. Her journey was far from over. She glanced at the front.

She saw the Cross of Christ still standing in its place. It never wavered from the weather. She was captivated by its presence. It invited her to come. She walked the center aisle as she did years ago. She noticed a small animal resting on its horizontal beam. She was comforted. Even the smallest of creatures know their Creator.

She remembered the first time she came to that cross. She was six years old. Her mother and father were separated. She believed she was to blame. She sought some type of peace and solace. She sought forgiveness. With her teddy bear in tow, she recalled walking slowly to the front. She knelt before the altar and gave her heart to the Lord. The peace she sought, she gained. The next day, her parents were together.

That feeling never left her. Now here she was again. The same issue that brought her to the front years ago brought her back: peace and forgiveness. She came to the front pews. There was a spot waiting for her. Unlike the other pews, this one remained clear and cleaned. It brightly shined as the sun rays pierced through the slats of the roof.

She sat. She was baffled by the spot next to her. It was also clear and clean. She wondered what it meant. She didn't know. She bowed her head a started to pray. Her prayer turned into floods of tears. The weight of everything was lifted. She was about to finish when she felt someone sit next to her. A hand took hold of hers. It was a hand she recognized so well. It was her mother's touch.

Carol did not look over, but rather looked up. "Thank you, Lord" she whispered.

Like her daughter, Maria sought for the same things and found them. She was transparent before her little girl. She broke down before the One who promised to carry her burdens. She couldn't control them. Though nothing was said between the two, everything was felt. For a church considered dead, this one was very much alive. For in that dark and dreary sanctuary was a healing service between a mother and her daughter.

CHAPTER TWENTY-SEVEN

Frank had his own issues. He was deeply concerned about Carol. In his absence, he feared the worse. He did not want her to suffer any more than she already had. Then again, Maria made it crystal clear that he was to keep his distance. He pondered her warning. She knew very well he and Carol attended the same school. To avoid her in the halls would be next to impossible.

Something did not settle right with him. Maria had another agenda. He was determined to figure it out and figure it out he did. He asked a simple question. How can two people attend the same school, walk the same hallways, and share the same classes without making contact? They can't. One person had to from the equation. That one person was Carol.

Frank panicked. He was frantic. He was confined. Part of his suspension was to remain in the house. Since he no longer had football practice, he had no reason to leave his home.

His second issue was soon to follow. He went to the kitchen. He found his parents sitting at the table. They had finished breakfast. They did not notice Frank's entrance. He wasted no time to let them know. "Did you know?" he shouted.

Kelly looked at Frank. His facial expressions complimented his feelings. "Did we know what?" she replied. Her voice was soft, subtle, and sincere.

"How Carol's mother has done everything to separate us," Frank desperately asked.

"Sweetheart," Kelly softly replied. "No, no went didn't."

His voice trembled. "I don't believe you! All of you have conspired against me and Carol."

"Let's back up a bit," Kelly said. "How has Maria separated you and Carol?"

"Last night she paid for my bail. She said my record would be cleared on two conditions. I pay for Scott's medical expenses and I pay no attention to Carol. She filed a restraining order against. Should I fail to honor her conditions, she would have me arrested."

"Oh she did, now did she?" Kelly shook her in disbelief. "I am not surprised. That's how Maria works. We had no idea who bailed you out. We thought you needed some time to settle down and cool off."

"You were going to leave me there?" Frank blurted. "I can't believe it! How dare you? What do you take me for, some criminal? I don't know who's the bitch, you are Maria.

Kelly's husband stepped in. He heard enough. "Don't talk to your mother in that fashion."

The years of neglect he suffered finally got the best of him. The volcano that lay dormant for years finally erupted. Frank exploded. No one was safe from the lava flow. In the end, everyone was singed and scarred.

Frank aimed his sights directly to his want-to-be-father. "Oh! Now you want to be the man of the house!" he spewed. Where were you when I needed you? When was the last time you showed any compassion or concern for me? That's right! I forgot. I'm not your son. Forgive me, won't you? Forgive me for who I am and what I have done. Forgive me for making your life so miserable! Forgive me…"

Kelly tried to extinguish the flames. She saw where her son was heading. "Frank! That's enough. No more!"

Though Frank saw his mother's lips moving, he heard nothing. He turned his attention to her. "Bullshit!" he shouted. "Where were you when I needed you? Let me guess, you were still banging Carol's father. How could you? What were you thinking? You think I need some time to myself, aren't you are calling the kettle black."

In a meager attempt to save what was lost, Kelly's husband interjected. "Let's call it a night before we say things we will later regret. Frank, go to your room!"

Those words triggered more seismic activity. Frank laughed. He used both hands to flip-off Kelly's husband. He struck, "I hope you can read sign language. Maria was right! If you were half the man everyone thought you were, we wouldn't be in this predicament. Would we?"

Kelly's husband challenged Frank. "You think I do not have the balls to take you down boy?"

"That's exactly what I am saying! Come on old man. I believe it's time for me to take you to school."

Testosterone levels were flying high. "You think?"

Frank smiled in anticipation. "I don't think, I know. Bring it on. When I am done, you will wish you were never born."

Kelly had enough. She jumped between the two men. "I have heard and seen enough! No more, it ends here. It ends now! If you are to hit anyone, let it be me!"

The magma flow finally ceased. The damage wrought on by the volcano had been done. Things would never be the same. Though casualties were few, the impact affected many.

CHAPTER TWENTY-EIGHT

Frank had enough. He felt trapped. He had to get out. He stormed for the door. Kelly's husband went to tackle him. "No, you don't. You are not leaving this house!" His meager attempt failed. Frank was too fast and strong.

Frank hit him senseless. "Watch me, old man!" Frank shouted. He struck him with such force that Kelly's husband sailed across the foyer and smashed against a wall. He staggered to get up. He tried to regain his ground, but it was too late. Frank was out of the house.

"Get your ass back in here young man or I will call the police!"

"Call them!" Frank thundered. He whipped to his car and soared in the wind. Nothing would stop him. Despite road conditions, he ripped through the streets. There was one person who would know about Carol. It was Lucy.

He raced to her house. He wasn't sure how to approach her. She did give him an upper-cut some days ago. In haste, he pulled into her driveway. He knocked on her door. Thankfully, Lucy answered. "What do you want?" she asked.

"I need your help," Frank said trembling.

Lucy sensed his sincerity. She saw it in his deep blue eyes. She heard it in his trembling voice. Intuitively, she knew something went terribly wrong. "How can I help? What can I do?" she begged.

"I am convinced Maria has taken Carol somewhere. Where? I don't know," he explained. I need you to confirm my suspicions."

"How?" she asked.

"I will drive you to their house. You can explain your concern for Carol. You stopped by to see how she was doing."

"And what if she is home?" Lucy inquired.

"Then I will know her mother has not thrown a curveball." Frank went on to say, "My gut says Carol won't be home."

"Okay!" Lucy agreed. "I will do it. I am not doing this for you; I am doing it for Carol."

"Understood," Frank said. "I appreciate your help."

"Give me a few moments to get dressed," Lucy replied. "I dare not go out looking like this."

Frank returned to his car. He waited for her. When she came out, she was stunning. She would any man's head turn. "WOW!" Frank thought. "Had I known she looked this good, she could punch me all day."

Lucy hopped in the car. She noticed Frank staring her down. "What?" she said.

"Nothing," Frank countered. "I have never seen you look..." he paused. He was caught. "I have never seen you look so dazzling."

"Stop joking around!" she said. She tried to redirect his attention. "Remember," she reminded him, "we are looking for Carol." Her efforts were in vain. Eventually, she would see in Frank what Carol saw. She was not quite sure. There was something about crystal blue eyes. They seemed to know everything about her. She resisted her temptation to kiss him with a gentle slap across his face. "We need to get going, don't you think?"

Her smack worked. Frank came to senses. "You are right. We need to find Carol."

CHAPTER TWENTY-NINE

Carol and Maria left the abandoned church. A relationship once severed was sutured. It was the cross of Christ that paved the way for reconciliation. They were reminded of His suffering and shame. They knew if Christ could endure the harshest of penalties, so too, could they. In fact, He demonstrated love at its finest moment.

Maria found it difficult to retrace her tracks. The snowdrifts continued to sweep across the landscape. Carol did not seem to mind. She and her mother's wounds were on the mend. Again, she waited for the perfect time to speak. It did not take long. The moment they were on the highway, they drove past another family memory. It was an old ice- cream stand. It was literally located in the land of nowhere. It stood by its lonesome on top of a long and winding road. That's what made it so appealing. Traveler's spotted it from afar.

Carol started to cry. The memories of time's past were as fresh as yesterday. "Mom," she cried with tears of joy, "do you remember how Dad always had to stop for ice cream?"

"Yes, I do?" she answered. "He always got the same thing: a chocolate peanut butter cone. Those were great times."

Overwhelmed by the thought, Carol burst into tears. "Oh Mom, I wish he were alive."

Carol opened up emotions Maria could no longer control or contain. She too joined in the orchestra of tears. "I miss him too," she cried. She couldn't see past her own tears. She went to pull off and park on the highway's shoulder when a semi-truck struck her in the rear. The impact sent the car into a tailspin. It flew over the guardrail and flipped into a ravine. There, by a frozen creek, in a ravine, off the highway, a mother and mother-to-be lay unconscious.

Emergency crews were quick to respond. Initially, they believed there were casualties. As fate would have it, both mother and daughter were very much alive. When one of the rescuers noticed Carol's condition, they anteed up their efforts. They resorted to every trick in the book to free them. A helicopter was called to life flight both women to the nearest hospital.

Midair, Maria regained consciousness. She looked to her right. She saw Carol lying motionless. She believed her daughter to be dead. She tried to reach for her, but couldn't. Her arms were restrained. The tears she showered earlier compared nothing to the ones she now shed. "No!" she tried to scream. "No! This can't be happening. Please don't take my babies."

Something caught her attention. Her prayers were answered. She saw life not so much in Carol but in Carol. She saw firsthand Carol's belly jump. The baby kicked.

CHAPTER THIRTY

Frank and Lucy drove to Carol's house. They were unaware of so many things: Maria's decision to relocate Carol and their accident along the highway. Fearing Maria's threat, Frank parked a block away. Lucy walked the rest of the way. She knocked on the door to see if Carol answered. Much to her dismay, no one answered. Even Lucy found that strange, considering all things. At first, she believed Carol went to school, but her suspicions were clouded when she noticed the two sets of footprints in the drive.

She also observed drag marks in the snow. They were somewhat fresh. The started from the front and ended where a car was parked. She knew something was pulled, but what? Lucy bent over. Whatever it was had wheels. She noticed marks scribbled on the sidewalk and drive. "Son of a bitch!" she said out loud. "Maria snapped. She kidnapped her own daughter. Shit! This is getting serious."

She ran back to Frank's car. She was out of breath. "They're gone!" she explained.

"What do you mean they're gone?" Frank said frantically. "Where would they go?"

Lucy was hysterical. "I don't know. Do I look like Sherlock Holmes? They left Dodge. That's all I know."

"That sucks! Now, what do we do?"

"You're asking the wrong person," Lucy said trembling. "I can't believe any of this. Take me home."

"We need to find them!" Frank shouted.

"Don't ever talk to me in that tone."

"Let me guess," he said half-heartedly. "You will throw another upper-cut."

"You are damn right. I am not your bitch. I never was, I never will be."

"Yes ma'am, as you wish." Frank started to pull his car from the curb when a special report interrupted the radio station. He was enraged. He had no time to hear about another person's problems. He had his own. He quickly flipped the station. Had he known, he would have thought twice. The report detailed Maria and Carol's accident. The questions Frank asked could have been answered.

He took Lucy home. He was at a loss for words. The thought that he may never see Carol or his baby was too much. He couldn't return to his house. Kelly and her husband were still there. He was barred from returning to school. He had nowhere to turn to or go. The last thing he desired was to be alone.

Lucy still had one day of suspension. Like Frank, she did want not to spend the day by herself either. She gazed into his blurry blue eyes and invited him in. He could not resist. He did not resist. He followed Lucy into her dwelling. The house was quiet. They were alone.

"Take a seat on the couch," Lucy said. "I can make something to eat."

"That's not necessary, I am not hungry." Frank looked pitiful. He was hurt and lost. Lucy sat next to him. She attempted to comfort him. His hurt was her hurt. She wiped away his tears. She ran her fingers through his hair. What started out as kind gestured turned into something serious. They could not restrain the temptations they felt earlier.

Before the morning expired, they were lying naked side by side. Lucy was firmly clutched in Frank's arms. He gently ran his hand down her spine. He started to caress her breasts. The emotional and physical fling they shared soon ended.

Lucy pushed Frank off of her. She pulled away and covered herself with a blanket. "Shit! We shouldn't be doing this. We can't be doing this," she yelped.

Frank was dumbfounded. "What? You did enjoy it, didn't you?"

"You are such a guy!" she blurted. "I don't know who is dumber than he looks you or the counselor. What about Carol? She is my best friend. She is pregnant with your child!"

His response proved an absolute that day. Frank was dumber than he looked. "Oh," he responded. "I guess you are right."

Lucy ordered Frank to get dressed and to go home. In as far as she was concerned, this never happened. Frank agreed. Had they known the outcome of their rendezvous, things may have ended differently.

CHAPTER THIRTY-ONE

Medics were quick to get Maria and Carol to the hospital. Maria was fully aware of what happened and her surroundings. She was more concerned for her daughter. She refused any treatment. She wanted to be with her daughter. Time was of the essence. Carol required immediate medical attention. The medics realized they would lose this battle. Maria would sign the necessary paperwork as long as she was present. The attending physicians complied. They wheeled both mother and daughter to the same room. One team examined Maria as other medical staff treated Carol.

Carol's vitals were of utmost importance. Doctor's hooked her up to a heart monitor, a blood-pressure cup, and an I. V. Maria paid no attention to what was being done to her. The moment Carol's heartbeat registered on the monitor, Maria pled for the baby. "She's pregnant!" She screamed. Maria started to spit-up blood. "My baby's carrying a baby!"

The staff x-rayed Maria's chest. She had three broken ribs. Her lung was punctured. Surgery was required. It was imminent. Her doctor instructed the team working on Carol to honor Maria's request.

An ultrasound was brought to the room. It was immediately hooked up and placed on Carol's womb. The images it produced brought Maria to tears. That was her grandchild. She saw almost everything. The child within her child was sucking his thumb. His arms and legs were easily visible. His head and eyes were distinguishable. He was a living being. Maria cried. "That's my daughter's baby!" she spat out. "Is it a boy or a girl?"

"Ma'am," the doctor said apologetically, "we need to get you into surgery."

"Is my grandchild a boy or girl, that's all I asking."

The surgeon appeased Maria. He bent over. He studied the images on the screen. "By all appearances, it's a boy!"

Maria reached out to Carol. She did not have the strength to touch her daughter let alone to speak. The anesthetics started to set in. "His name," she mumbled, "is Zachary Taylor." She was immediately wheeled to the surgical room.

Carol, on the other hand, sustained several bruises and lacerations. She finally woke up. She had no memory of the accident or anything that happened thereafter. Her last recollection was the ice-cream stand atop the long and winding road. A nurse came in when Carol first opened her eyes. "Where am I?" she softly asked.

"Honey," the nurse replied, "you are in the hospital."

"How did I get here? What happened?" Carol grimaced.

"You were in a car accident. Outside of some cuts and bruises, you will be fine."

Carol's pain was evident. Her concern was more geared towards her child. "Did they check on my baby?"

"Yes," the nurse smiled, "he's doing fine. He has a strong mother."

"It's a he?" Carol asked.

The nurse confirmed Carol's suspicions. "Yes, we did an ultrasound. You are definitely having a boy."

Carol perked up. "I knew it," she said confidently. "His name is Zachary Taylor."

"That's a beautiful name. What made you decide on that name."

"My dad," Carol responded. "He loved history. Of all the presidents, Zachary Taylor was his favorite."

"Oh!" the nurse surprisingly said. "My apologies: I do not know history that well. Zachary Taylor served as president?"

"He did," Carol said with confidence. "He was our twelfth president. He was a major general during the Mexican-American wars. He was considered a hero to most. His reputation on the battlefield earned him the presidency. He died sixteen months into his term. He wanted to preserve the Union from the growth of slavery."

"They say you learn something new every day," the nurse responded with a smile. "Your father seems like a wise man."

"He was a wise man," Carol shared. "He was a caring man. He was the best. That is until he took his own life."

"I am so sorry," the nurse said. She tried to contain her tears, but couldn't. "I can't imagine your grief," she added.

"No, no you can't. I believe he ended his life because of me." Carol cried.

"I have a hard time believing that you were the cause of his death. From what I heard, it seems that you gave your father the strength to live as long as he did."

Carol never looked at her father's tragedy in those terms. "I imagine so," she faintly said. "How's my mother doing?"

"She's recovering from surgery. She suffered some broken ribs along with a punctured lung. She should be up and about in the next day or two."

"Can I see her?" Carol wanted to know.

"Maybe tomorrow," the nurse answered. "She is still weak from the surgery."

"Does she know about my baby?" Carol paused. "Does she know he is a boy?"

"She knows," the nurse laughed, she refused to go into surgery until she found out."

CHAPTER THIRTY-TWO

Months passed since the accident. Maria sold her home. She and Carol started a new life in a new town. Carol continued with her pregnancy. From all counts, "Little Zachary" was a healthy baby boy. Her doctor earned Carol's confidence. They often spoke for hours about options. If Carol learned anything from dating a star quarterback, it was the ability to change a play on the line of scrimmage. She and her doctor discussed what to do if the "what if's" took place. They studied the playbook religiously.

Frank was at a loss. He passed by Carol's house every day. Every day he saw the same "For Sale" sign sitting in the yard. Maria kept her promise. So too did Scott's parents. He was not charged with "felonious assault." His record was expunged. He did receive his scholarship. He was headed for the "Big Ten." Kelly and her husband were proud of his accomplishments. The counselor proved right. "Character was not defined by what a person does, but what he does to correct the wrongs."

Lucy, on the other hand, was not faring so well. She was not her old self. She felt weak. She was nauseated. She was late. To ease her mind, she bought a home pregnancy test. Much to her dismay and surprise, she was indeed pregnant. She feared the worst. She did not want to suffer the humiliation as Carol. She did not know who to go to or what to do. Frank was the father.

She did everything she could to hide it, but time was not on her side. Each day her clothes were tighter and the "baby bump" continued to grow. Students chided her by her sudden weight gain. They even went so far as to joke about her condition. They continued their verbal assaults with each passing day. It was not uncommon for her to hear words like, "What's that bump in your belly? It's a baby!" or "Was Carol your teacher?"

Frank heard the rumors circulating. He couldn't believe it. "How could he allow this to happen a second time?" he thought. "Now, what was he to do?" His first instincts were to own up to it. He needed to be a man. Yet, there were those thoughts to ignore her situation. How was he to know that it was his child? "He was not" he reasoned, "Lucy's first. Why should he take the blame for another man's actions?"

Despite his best efforts to block his sexual encounter of the third kind with Lucy, he couldn't. It was his. He literally screwed up twice in one year. He remembered Carol's ultrasound. He remembered everything he studied about a baby's development. Sadly, he followed in the footsteps of his and Carol's father. Ironically, he knew all these things but didn't know what to do.

Lucy answered his questions. It was the morning of their dress rehearsal. Graduation was the following evening. Carol had Maria call Lucy about her whereabouts and her condition. Carol was only two hours away and was very much in labor.

Frank was getting out of his car when Lucy ordered him to get back in. "We are going on a road trip," she spouted. He was caught off-guard. He completely forgot Carol's due date. "Where are we going?" he questioned. "We are getting ready to graduate tomorrow."

"Trust me, this far more important. I believe you need to be there." Lucy said.

Frank proved to be dumber than he looked. "What could be more important than graduation?"

Lucy gave him a sign. She held onto her belly. "I will give you one guess, you dumbass."

His eyes went wide right. He saw Lucy's baby taking shaping. "It's Carol, isn't it?"

"Duh?" she said. "You need, I mean, we need to be there."

Frank's emotions got the best of him. "It would help if you told me where I was going?"

Lucy looked at him. "What did I tell you months ago?"

He shrugged his shoulders. "I don't remember."

She did not stutter. "I am not your bitch, so don't treat me like one! By the way," she went on to add, "I am carrying your child. I would appreciate some sympathy from this child's father."

Lucy left Frank speechless. His worse fears were confirmed. He was responsible for two children. He was no different from his father. Confusion filled him. "What do you want me to say? What if Carol notices? What then?"

"Carol does not need to know," Lucy said. "She has enough on her mind at this time. Hopefully, she won't say anything."

"And if she does?" Frank inquired.

"I will have your back," she affirmed. "I will confirm that you are not the father."

"Thank you," he replied. "Where are we going?"

"We are traveling due East. Carol is closer than you think."

CHAPTER THIRTY-THREE

C arol was in labor. Maria sat by her side. Doctor's monitored her. Carol, like most first time mothers, experienced a long and arduous labor. Though her water broke hours ago, she was dilated three centimeters. The pains of labor were sporadic and unpredictable. She cried. Her tears were of joy more than anything else.

Her gynecologists periodically checked on her. She poked and prodded. "Well, it looks like "Little Zachary" is taking his time. That's to be expected."

Carol was showing signs of concern. "How is he doing?"

The doctor studied the monitors. "Your son is doing fine. His heart rate is normal. He is not under any stress. There's no reason to worry," the doctor added. "Firstborn's usually take the longest."

Maria clasped Carol's hand. "You will be fine, I promise."

Her words were muffled by Frank and Lucy's appearance. They walked into the room. Carol was shocked to see Frank more so than Lucy. "What brings you here?" she asked.

"You are having our son!" Frank responded. "I have every right to be here."

"Really," Carol shot back. "Where have you been? What my baby needs is a father, not a sperm donor!"

Frank did not hesitate to answer her. "Ask your mother," he fired. "She's the one who separated us. She's the one who threatened to have me arrested if I came close to you! She's the one you need to question, not me."

Carol diverted her attention to Maria. "Mom, is that true?"

With Carol's hand still in her grasp, Maria admitted to her wrongdoings. "Yes, he is telling you the truth. I posted bail for him under the condition he no longer had anything to do with you."

"Why? What would make you do such a thing?" Carol demanded.

"I was only thinking about your best interest. I didn't want us to share the same experience. After our accident, I totally forgot about my conversation with him."

"You were involved in an accident?" Frank blurted out. He turned his blue eyes to Maria. "And what makes you think I had no reason to know?"

"Young man," Maria fired back. "It's none of your business. You are forgetting one thing. I am her mother."

Frank went on the defensive. "Yes, you are her mother, but she's pregnant with my child."

Maria did what Maria did best. She was a bitch. "That's your story." She happened to glance at Lucy. She noticed the "baby bump." "Let me guess," she chided. She pointed to Lucy's abdomen. "That's your baby too!"

Carol redirected her attention to Lucy. She saw the same thing. Lucy was pregnant. She interrogated her best friend. "Is it true? Are you pregnant?"

Lucy refused to admit to any wrongdoing. "I don't know what you are talking about. So I gained some weight. What business is it of yours?"

"My mother is correct," Carol argued. "You are pregnant. Carol snapped her finger to Frank. Is it his?"

The spotlight was now on Lucy. She tried to divert the conversation. She felt trapped. She was caught. She became extremely anxious. Sweat started to bead from her head. Her heart raced. "At this point, does it really matter?"

"You are damn right it matters," Carol shouted. "I asked a question. A simple 'yes' or 'no' would have sufficed. But I suppose that was too complicated. I can't believe I considered you my best friend. What was I thinking?"

"It was an accident," Lucy tried to explain. "It just happened. We were emotionally stripped of your whereabouts."

"By the looks of things, you were stripped by other things." Before she continued her spill, her doctor walked in. "Excuse," she politely said, "I need you two to leave the room."

Frank and Lucy stepped out. An argument ensued. "I told you this was a bad idea," he whispered.

"How did I know her mother would notice my baby bump?" She argued.

"How couldn't she? It's not as well-hidden as you think. Trust me, everyone in school knows. For weeks, they have ridden my back claiming it's mine."

Lucy jabbed her finger into Frank's chest. "For the record, it is your baby. Do you take me for some kind of slut or tramp?"

"No! I never thought that." His words were getting louder.

"Your friends told me a different story." Her finger jab was getting stronger with each word." "They said you denied any involvement with me. They also say you attacked my character by giving me the nickname 'Loosely,' instead of Lucy. Besides, how am I to think when you have avoided me like the plague?"

Frank sought a way out. "We are here for Carol, okay? You found me, I didn't find you. Can we talk about this later?"

Lucy rolled her eyes. "Like that is going to do anything."

CHAPTER THIRTY-FOUR

The commotion caused the baby's heart to race erratically. Carol went from three centimeters to eight in a short time. "Little Zachary" was indeed in distress.

"Carol," her doctor explained, "I need to know if you want to do an audible. If you are going to change the play, now's the time!"

Carol's mind spiraled out of control. Her thoughts consumed her. Everything flashed before her eyes. Her father's suicide wanted to rush across the lines. Her unexpected pregnancy sought to strip her of control. Her incestuous relationship with Frank wanted to jump off-sides. Her mother's warnings of would and could happen barked over the crowds. Frank's absence and Lucy's pregnancy showed signs of an oncoming blitz.

The doctor stood on the sideline. "Honey!" she shouted. "I really need to know before it's too late. Are you changing the play?"

"Yes," Carol screamed. Her contractions grew stronger and longer.

"Listen to me," the doctor said. "The baby's crown is soon to break through! Once it does it will be too late."

Carol changed the play. She yelled through her pain, "Blue-34! Blue-34!"

The surgeon wasted no time. She ordered Maria to leave the room. "You must go! You must go now!"

Maria was in a state of shock! "I have every right to be present. I am the grandmother."

"Ma'am, at present," the doctor ordered, "under the law, you have no rights. I need you to leave now!"

"That's not going to happen!" she shot back. "That's my grandson you are delivering."

"It's your daughter's son! She had made her decision, and I need you to leave."

Maria was not budging. She feared the worst. She feared "Little Zach" would be aborted. "I'm not leaving!"

"Yes you are," the surgeon said. "Security, remove this person from the premises. We don't have all day."

A guard complied, "As you wish." He took Maria by the arms and escorted her to the hall.

"Carol," Maria begged. "Don't! Please don't terminate your pregnancy!"

It was too late. The playbook had changed. Carol, in the end, made the final call. For Maria, Frank, and Lucy, they were never given the details of what happened and how it happened. The last thing they heard was Carol's life-giving scream to push. Outside of that, all was quiet.

When the surgeon left the berthing area, she was asked about Carol's and the baby's condition. She did everything to cushion the shock from what transpired. "You should be able to see Carol in an hour or so?"

Frank finally manned up. "What about "Little Zach? I am his father. I have a right to know."

The surgeon shook her head. "Young man," she said apologetically, "no you don't. The law favors the mother's rights over yours."

"Can I at least see him?" Frank cried.

"I'm sorry," the surgeon answered. "His little body now belongs to the State. I wish there was more for me to say, but Carol's rights and privacy are protected by law. Now, if you would excuse me, I have other babies to deliver."

CPSIA information can be obtained
at www.ICGtesting.com
Printed in the USA
FFHW01n1225211018
48907023-53140FF